DEVON GHOSTS

By Theo Brown

ISBN 0-8530-6961-1
© *Jarrold Publishing 1982*
Published by Jarrold Publishing, Norwich
First published 1982
Reprinted 1992
Printed in Great Britain 2/92

Introduction

I have always noticed that the best ghost stories are those one cannot hope to make use of; generally speaking the existence of ghosts can never be proved to the satisfaction of everyone, so it is hardly surprising if the only person who accepts the experience as genuine is the percipient himself, but he keeps it to himself for fear of ridicule. Also, many are of so intimate a nature that the percipient shrinks from talking about it. Hence it rarely happens that one gets the story 'hot from the oven'; sometimes it is buried deep in the mind for years. But it niggles and disturbs. People have told me of experiences that happened many years ago and often the telling is a great release of anxiety and doubt enabling an irrational event to be integrated in the memory. But in such circumstances one cannot pass on any identifiable details. So, in most cases I have changed the names of my informants and have even suppressed the name of the locality on occasion.

Devon has its full share of haunted houses, but even when the occupiers are quite happy with their spectral tenants they do not always like it noised abroad, being under the impression that it devalues the property. On the other hand, many home-seekers deliberately ask for a house with a ghost; a house-agent assures me that a good ghost will add £1,000 to the asking price. It is a delicate problem: many informants will talk quite cheerfully about their ghosts but do not want them publicised.

Of course, there are many different kinds of ghosts; some are seen or heard quite regularly; some are only spotted by sensitive psychics; some are traditional but have 'worn out', as it were, with the passage of time; some attached to known historical subjects are mere folk-memories coloured by myth and are never seen. Hence, while I have known people who have the rather unenviable gift of seeing scenes from the past at almost any place, the majority of ghost stories are to be classed as folktales.

Within a few miles of Exeter are several notoriously haunted houses I could name; but they have changed hands so frequently (having been schools, hotels or nursing homes in rapid succession since the last war) that it would be tactless to identify them. Some boast several active ghosts, others only one, or occasional poltergeist demonstrations.

What is surprising is that some ancient homes, which look as though they should be crawling with spectres of all kinds, prove to be completely void of such residents. Which brings me to a point I want to make. Real ghosts (that is the kind that someone claims to have seen, heard or smelt) seldom, if ever, have a story attached to them. Someone, not necessarily psychic, sees a man in the doorway, who is there, and then vanishes – and that is all there is to him. Take, for example, 'William', who is seen in a vicarage at odd times by the family. Nothing whatever is known about him, he is quiet and friendly and no one is frightened by him. He is just there! Disappointing for an author in search of good stories. Of course, there are plenty of romantic ghost stories in Devon as elsewhere, but these characters are seldom seen, if ever. As a recent BBC talk put it, most English ghosts are 'episodic'; the more detailed the supposed history, the less likely it is to be genuine, and they follow conventional patterns, some of which I have dealt with in my *The Fate of the Dead*, published by the Folklore Society in 1979.

Obviously any place where people have been at any time in history – or before – may have left an impression that may be manifested as a haunting. It is simply a matter of discovering the circumstances that will trigger off phenomena. Possibly lighting and weather conditions have a lot to do with it. In so many cases we seem to be eavesdropping on a past scene; similar conditions would make this easier, just as certain moments in spring and autumn suddenly bring back our own memories so vividly.

I have tried in this book to give as wide a selection as possible, taken from a mountain of material. I owe a very great debt of gratitude to those householders who have so freely and generously allowed me to mention their hauntings. Many of my stories have been published by the Devonshire Association, in my Report on Folklore, given annually for the past thirty years, and I am most grateful to the Council and Honorary Editor for allowing me to make use of this source, and also to the Honorary Editor of *Devon and Cornwall Notes and Queries* where much of the more mythical material has been published.

I have in many cases altered or suppressed personal names, and would like to point out that though I have usually given the place-name this does not mean that houses are open to the public. My good friends would not appreciate the invasion of their privacy any more than you would if your house suddenly sprang a poltergeist.

I do especially want to thank the Committee and Librarian of the Devon and Exeter Institution for allowing us to make use of their wonderful collection of old topographical prints and also all those friends and colleagues who have helped in numerous ways, especially my publishers who have been so patient.

Finally, I should explain and perhaps apologise for some imbalance in the length of sections. It is natural that one notices and records most efficiently the stories found near home. All collectors suffer from this and there seems little one can do except to utilise this factor. It would be impossible to cover a vast county like Devon evenly, and it would be foolish to imitate Procrustes and lop off good stories simply because one has heard them since early youth. Hence the sections on South and East Devon and the Exeter area are disproportionately long, though I could easily have doubled the length of each.

Contents

INTRODUCTION

SOUTH DEVON
Barton Hall Area (*Kingskerswell, etc.*)	10
The John Lee Mystery (*Babbacombe*)	15
The Haunted Organ (*Torquay*)	18
The Bishop Takes a Hand (*Abbotskerswell, nr Newton Abbot*)	19
Bradley Manor (*Newton Abbot*)	20
Oldstone (*Blackawton*)	22
The Hole in the Path (*Yealmpton*)	24
The Weaver and the Parson (*Dean Prior*)	26
The Hound of the Baskervilles (*Buckfastleigh*)	29
Berry Pomeroy Castle	33
The White Lady of Dartington	35

EXETER AND DISTRICT
Exeter and District	38
The Ghost of Mr Kingdon (*Exeter*)	39
Queen Henrietta Maria	40
A Haunted Church? (*Withycombe Ralegh*)	43
Fontelautus Dennis (*Exmouth*)	45

Theo Brown's 'Shadow' 46
The Great Devon Mystery (*Torquay to Littleham*) 47
The Sokespitch Barrel (*Clyst St George*) 53

EAST DEVON
The Sampford Peverell Ghost 56
A Ghost Scare in Plymtree (*nr Cullompton*) 58
The Witch of Membury (*nr Axminster*) 60
The Bleeding Hawk of Hillersdon (*Cullompton*) 63

NORTH DEVON
The White Bird of the Oxenhams
  (*Zeal Monachorum nr Okehampton*) 66
Eight Hundred Years After the Murder
  (*Lapford and Woolacombe Sands*) 68
The Bathe Pool (*North Tawton*) 71
A Story of Something . . . (*Lynton area*) 72
The Demon of Spraiton (*Spreyton*) 75
The White Hart Hotel (*Okehampton*) 78

WEST DEVON
A Haunted House in Plymouth 80
The Accursed Field at Stowford
  (*between Lifton and Okehampton*) 81
Betsy Grimbal of Tavistock 82
Frithelstock Priory (*nr Great Torrington*) 84
Drake's Drum (*Buckland Monachorum*) 87
The Haunted Rectory (*Luffincott*) 89

HAUNTED ROADS
Haunted Roads 92
The Hairy Hands (*Postbridge*) 95
Jay's Grave (*nr Hound Tor, Dartmoor*) 99
A Warning to Travellers (*Roborough Down*) 102

ANIMAL GHOSTS
Horses 104

    Pigs 106
    Lamb and Goat 108
    Some Nasty Cats 109
    Foxes and Hares 111
    Black Dogs 113
    Whisht Hounds 120

A MISCELLANY OF DEVON GHOSTS
    Some Throw-Backs 122
    Phantom Houses 124
    Reginald de Mohun (*Torquay*) 126
    The 'Dream Church' (*Milber, nr Newton Abbot*) 127
    Pixies 128
    Sealed Rooms – and Their Occupants 134
    Haunted Waters 137
    Cutty Dyer (*Ashburton*) 141

South Devon

Barton Hall Area
The John Lee Mystery
The Haunted Organ
The Bishop Takes a Hand
Bradley Manor, Newton Abbot
Oldstone, Blackawton
The Hole in the Path, Yealmpton
The Weaver and the Parson, Dean Prior
The Hound of the Baskervilles, Buckfastleigh
Berry Pomeroy Castle
The White Lady of Dartington

Barton Hall Area

This was my home for the first twenty-one years of my life. It was built by my great-grandfather on virgin soil sometime between 1830 and 1840 to the plans of Gribble, one of the well-known Victorian Gothic architects. The house was designed in mock Tudor style with a magnificent moulded porch, vast cellars, two towers and two triangular strong-rooms with steel doors. One room had a window over a marble mantelpiece: a trick feature I have only seen elsewhere at Rougemont House in Exeter and at Powderham Castle. As is common with such houses, it was full of awkwardly shaped rooms and niches. Over the central hall is a skylight, which tradition said was the death of one of the builders who fell from the scaffolding.

I remember it mainly for its draughts and leaking leads. Otherwise it was fun, and ideal for hide-and-seek. I do not think it was haunted in any way, and if it had been there were always enough young people to frighten away any number of bogeys, but this never stopped odd stories getting around. I think this was largely because my father kept bloodhounds and peacocks, who on occasion set up their peculiar noises that sounded most eery to passers-by on the road at night-time. There was also an occasional nestful of baby white owls in the deserted stables, hissing loudly for their supper! As it was surrounded by woods, the house with its pseudo-Gothic appearance and tall chimneys could look very creepy against the evening sky.

With all this it is hardly surprising that soon after the last war, when it first became a holiday camp, the story got around that the Hall had been built on the site of a pre-Reformation nunnery, and that the old library, then converted into an office, had been the chapel – this on the strength of a plaster vaulted ceiling and an oddly shaped marble wash-hand basin! Moreover, a journalist added the ghost of a headless nun! When I reported this to a folklore colleague, she pondered thoughtfully, 'I wonder when someone will *see* her!' Some years later I heard locally that another ghost had now joined the party: this time the spirit of a maidservant who had been betrayed by a footman and had committed suicide. I much doubt whether anyone remotely resembling a footman had ever been employed there.

My parents were sensible about ghosts: that is, they believed in them on principle but were not unduly disturbed. My mother was psychic and could sense anything unusual in her surroundings, but she was a good Christian woman and held that nothing could harm you if you put your trust in God. My father had served in a Scottish regiment for twenty-five years and had been a welcome guest in many Highland castles and houses and was steeped in Scottish family traditions. Though he took a sturdily extrovert view of it all, he nevertheless admitted the possibility of mysteries outside his ken. None of us living at Barton ever thought there was anything spooky about the place, but we accepted there were haunted spots nearby.

The family vault under the high altar in Kingskerswell parish church, for instance, held one coffin which, whenever the vault was opened to receive a new resident, was always found to be lying on the top step. This was the coffin containing an outsider, that is, a non-Brown. He was Colonel Richard Ellicombe who had married one of the Brown women. They had resided at the old Manor House; she had died first, in 1782. The widower lived on alone, a fat disagreeable old man who loathed little boys and pigs, and in old age actually boasted that he had never seen a boy or a pig in his life without hitting it. Not the most popular member of the family or the local community. He died in 1804 and joined his wife in the vault, much to the fury of the family, living and dead. Those of the family in the crypt so much resented his presence that they constantly attempted to push him out, so that his coffin was always found lying on the topmost step whenever the vault was opened. Of course, as my father used to observe, the vault does get flooded sometimes, and maybe the coffin is airtight and floats – but who would want to spoil a good story!

Two lanes near us were haunted; both led off from Kerswell Cross. One came up a steep hill from Scott's Bridge on the Newton–Torquay road, by the new roundabout for the ring road to Brixham. Near the top of the short hill, as the lane levelled out, there was said to be a haunted field. This was on the slope below the spot where my father picked up some flint arrowheads.

In about 1935 he wrote of this place: 'When I was a boy I was told by my father that a manservant was sent one night into Torquay on a pony to get something. He came up Scott's Bridge at about 10.30 p.m. It was a very dark night, and when he got about half way up the lane the pony stopped dead and refused to move. At the same time he saw a white figure on the gate of a field on his right-hand side. Do what he would, it was a very long time before he could get the pony past this gate with the figure on it, but at last it bolted and came home at a full

Barton Hall, c.1921

gallop. The man was much frightened and fainted on his arrival. Nothing would ever induce the pony to go down that lane again; also, as a boy I remember that no poacher would send a dog into the field. If they did it rushed out screaming as if something had got hold of it. I myself used to keep bloodhounds, and I often went with one of them down this lane, but every now and then at a certain place the hound would stop and start baying. Every hound I ever had did this, and always in the same place. I have frequently been over both hedges on these occasions, but I never found anyone there at all.'

At Kerswell Cross this lane continues on towards Coffinswell, a mile away, across a wide valley and water meadows, a glory of primroses and 'flags' in summer. This valley is also said to be haunted. My father wrote of it:

'Willowpark Lane crosses a stream, and the Vicar told me he had frequently heard people talking just as he came to this stream; he also had gone into the fields each side of the lane on these occasions but he never found anyone there. One Sunday evening in the autumn I was returning from church. I was late and walking very fast. Just as I came down the steep hill, on the Coffinswell side of the valley I saw a man and a dog about seventy yards in front of me. I was travelling faster than them and got up to within about three yards of them. They went round a sharp bend in the lane – and absolutely vanished! The hedges here were both seven and eight feet high: it was impossible that they could have got over them in anything under thirty or forty seconds, and I was not two seconds behind them.

'The man was very thick set and had on breeches and gaiters, with a brown tailed coat and a billy-cock hat. The dog, which was about the size of a sheep dog, baffles all description. I was so close to the man's back that I could see the seam of his coat, but the dog was closer. I did not feel at all alarmed. . . .'

Further on, my father's notes continue:

'Very many roads near the coast of Devon were considered to be haunted. This was in great measure caused by the smugglers, so as to keep the public indoors at night. At Brixham there was a man who took the brandy inland: this he did with a hearse painted with phosphorus; the horses had their feet padded in order to travel quietly, and the driver was got up as the Devil himself. When this conveyance was on the road everybody fled from it in terror.'

It is remembered in Paignton that the horses' heads were sometimes covered with black sacks to make them appear headless! Between Barton Hall and Kerswell Cross there is a very ancient and battered hollow oak, standing in a field by the edge of the wood called Kilpark, and looking towards Dartmoor. 'The Brandy Bottle Tree' was used as a cache by smugglers landing kegs at Watcombe – and this well into the nineteenth century. It was a clever ploy of the villains to make full use of local superstitions and even invent a few to make sure the way was clear of loiterers.

My father said that nothing would induce anyone to walk from St Marychurch to Shaldon after dark, as the road was haunted by 'Spring Hill Jack' – obviously a local adaptation of the ubiquitous and harmful 'Spring Heel Jack' of Victorian London – who used to dance about on the road and leap over the hedges each side with the greatest of ease. I can think of two other places in Devon favoured by a similar character. He also told me that balls of fire were said to roll out of the hedges in front of people who ventured there at night. One wonders how this was engineered.

Of course, as a youngster one listened eagerly to the conversation at table and took the keenest interest in ghost stories about places and people one knew; indeed one heard some strange tales from the

St Mary's Church, Kingskerswell

Torquay and South Devon area, which is why I have included rather a large proportion of South Devon stories in this little book. There were rumours of haunted houses, particularly one which was never named and which had something really awful in it. Sometimes a black dog was seen. One night a woman living there put her hand out of bed and felt a human head with curly hair there, but, alas, one seldom heard of the outcome of such nastinesses. I have wondered whether this particular house could have been Castel-la-Mare in the Warberries, the house whose horrific haunting was made famous by the writings of Beverley Nicholls and Violet Tweedale. This dreadful place was demolished in 1920.

At Watcombe, not far from us, was Rock House, which Rudyard Kipling and his wife rented in 1896. They left because they both became aware of a 'brooding Spirit of deep, deep Despondency' which they found quite insupportable, as he described in *Something of Myself* which he published forty years later.

The John Lee Mystery

Babbacombe beach lies at the bottom of a very steep cliff. For the infirm and the lazy there has been a funicular railway for many years, but in the last century it was a somewhat isolated spot, unspoilt by numerous amateur naturalists collecting specimens yet with just enough space for a few houses to be built above the high-tide mark. One of these was inhabited by a certain Mrs Keyse, who in her younger days had been to Court and had hobnobbed with the highest in the land. She kept several servants and frequently entertained royalty and friends of her London days. One of her servants was John Lee, aged 22, a young footman whom she had taken on despite a prison record for theft.

On 16 November 1884 the house was found to be on fire and Mrs Keyse was discovered dead from a fractured skull and cut throat. Nothing had been stolen, but young John Lee, the footman, having a criminal record, was the obvious suspect and he was arrested. He was tried at Exeter and condemned to be hanged on 23 February 1885. He insisted throughout he was innocent. On his last night he dreamt that the trap would three times fail to function, next morning. And in fact this happened exactly as he had dreamt it, although in the horror of the event he forgot the dream till later, never having taken it seriously. The lever and timbers were adjusted and two more attempts were made to hang him – three in all. Then the chaplain intervened and persuaded the Governor to postpone the execution. Eventually this was commuted to a life sentence. When he had completed a number of years of the sentence he was released and married a nurse from Newton Hospital, moving to another part of the country. I can remember that popular opinion considered the woman was crazy to take him on.

This macabre affair gave birth to a great deal of folklore. The crowd watching outside Exeter Gaol saw a flock of doves hovering over the execution yard and believed this proved Lee's innocence, while the trap failing to work was the result of divine intervention.

Others believed that it was the result of witchcraft. Lee's old grandmother, who lived at Ogwell, was thought to have strange powers. When it was learnt that Lee was to be executed, neighbours who ventured to commiserate with old Granny Lee all received the same answer: 'They won't hang him.' And Miss Estelle Dunsford heard the following tradition:

'Before dawn on the day he was to be hung, Granny Lee was seen to leave her cottage and set out towards Exeter. She walked there and took up a position on Rougemont overlooking the prison.

'All day she kept vigil there, never moving or taking her eyes from the prison. Then at evening she tramped back home.

'The village people firmly believed that the failure of the trap to work was due to the power of Granny Lee's spell.

'When she got home that night she told my informant's grandmother that he was safe – they would not be able to harm him now.'

An even stranger version came my way some years ago, from an old man who used to live on the Barton Hall Estate. His name was William Brown (no relation), and his grandmother was a friend, perhaps a kinswoman, of John Lee's mother. It transpires that John Lee's half-sister was also a servant in Mrs Keyse's house, and one of the visitors from London took a fancy to the girl. He used to slip into the kitchen at night-time, as the old lady went to bed early. However, one night she suddenly came down to speak to John:

'When she opened the door and saw what was going on and recognised someone high up, she dropped in a faint. Then someone was afraid of the scandal and got the idea of burning, etc., and was going to let John take the rap and be hung, but someone told someone higher again, and to clear someone, the hanging was rigged.'

In other words, the gentleman in the kitchen would quite happily have let Lee hang, only someone, perhaps Lee's mother, showed signs of making trouble, so the gallows was fixed *not* to work. A most unlikely story, but my informant had heard that the affair caused Queen Alexandra to refuse ever to visit Torquay. . . .

William Brown even suggested that the cover-up was staged by the Freemasons, though this was merely his own idea and had no basis in fact.

Lord Halifax's Ghost Book, 1936, pp. 159–63.
A. C. Ellis: *An Historical Survey of Torquay*, 1930, p. 320.

John Lee – 'The man they couldn't hang'.

St John's Church

The Haunted Organ

One of the more imposing churches in Torquay is St John's, overlooking the harbour. It was built in 1867 to replace a smaller chapel-of-ease to Torre parish church. It is heavily decorated, with coloured marbles, a mural and a window by Burne-Jones. At the back of the church, its huge rectangular font has steps leading down for total immersion. On the tower is an illuminated cross which at night shines out over Torbay. This was given in memory of Cyril Maude, the well-known actor-manager, who retired to Torquay and worshipped in St John's. I was present at the dedication in 1955.

In 1956, it was decided to replace the old organ, for a rather curious reason. It was in very bad repair – and it was haunted. The Vicar, the late Father Anthony Rouse, told me that a previous organist, a young man called Henry Ditton Newman, died in 1883. While his body lay in the church before the funeral, one of the congregation keeping watch heard the organ playing by itself. This parishioner was, by strange coincidence, a woman who had taught me at my first school and was still living, though obviously of a great age. I knew Father Rouse slightly and talked to him over the telephone; he was very busy at that moment: soon after he moved to another parish and died suddenly, so I had no opportunity of discussing the matter further. The old organ had frequently been heard by various people since the death of the young organist. Just what tune it played I could not discover. We all know that organs, if there is some wind left in them, will spontaneously play an odd note or so, but apparently this one was played by invisible hands. One would much like to know whether the ghost has accompanied it to its new resting place.

The Bishop Takes a Hand

Some years ago, in 1963, there was quite a stir, which was sympathetically reflected in the media, about a haunted house just off the main road from Newton Abbot to Torquay. This was Aller House, a large rather prosaic Victorian-Georgian edifice converted into flats. One of these was occupied by a young couple who had recently moved in. They complained that furniture was being moved around preternaturally, and that the wireless was liable to be switched on when there was no one around. The neighbour in the next flat could hear the noise. Sometimes heavy footsteps were heard, and odd things seen, such as a white mist moving through the flat. The occupants concluded the place must be haunted, but could find out nothing in the history of the house to account for it, unless, perhaps, it was the aftermath of a suicide which had occurred somewhere in the vicinity fifty years before.

Eventually the then Bishop of Exeter was consulted. Dr R. C. Mortimer was interested in such phenomena and had gathered a small group of clergy to assist him in certain kinds of difficult cases like this. He visited Aller House and, as was his custom, commenced by blessing the members of the household. This produced a marked reaction on the part of one person, and all noted an inexplicable drop in temperature, a common occurrence in haunted houses. Then the Bishop exorcised the house and the atmosphere at once lightened and cleared.

But a few days later there was a new development. The people living in the next flat found themselves landed with a ghost, 'the figure of a rather good-looking young man dressed in Edwardian clothes, wearing a stiff collar with turned-down points and bow tie.' The ghost had evidently been driven out of one flat into another by the exorcism. It never did anything; it was just there and caused no offence, so it was left in peace. But the house was in a bad condition, and not long afterwards was abandoned and demolished.

Bradley Manor

Bradley Manor, Newton Abbot

This is a medieval manor house believed to be one of the finest examples of its kind in Devon. The oldest part dates back to about 1250. The land there has been occupied since Neolithic times, and on the hill behind it is a late Iron Age camp. Concerning this, the occupier, Mrs Diana Woolner, F.S.A., the well-known archaeologist, told me the local story that on moonlit nights, if you go up to the entrance, you can see dead men lying around, which would seem to be the psychic echo of a battle.

Bradley Manor itself (now National Trust property) is a house of great charm, lying in a wooded valley, just off the Newton Abbot–Totnes road. Behind the house the ground rises slightly to form a very delightful lawn; this used to be a courtyard enclosed by a range of stables, which were demolished about 1750. Mrs Woolner wrote in 1954:

'Sometime last summer an elderly woman came to see our house. She was interested, as her family had lived in the neighbourhood.

'When she was shown the site of the former courtyard or triangle west of the Great Hall, she volunteered the information that the far side (i.e. the west wing of the courtyard) was the stables. This information was then unknown to her guide though known to me from an independent tradition. My father was told it in about 1912 by an old man who knew about the foundations being finally cleared away to make the garden. The woman then volunteered the following information.

'Her grandmother had been in service at Bradley Manor, and had been told that the old stables were haunted. So badly were they haunted that they were fallen into ruin (apparently through disuse). They were visited by the ghost of a young man, the son of the house, who had been killed out riding, and who ever after haunted the stables where his horse had returned. In the end the old stables had been pulled down. That was all the story.'

It is thought that the ghost must have been one of the Yarde family who owned the house for a long time before selling it about 1750. The stables were said to be of the Tudor period and coins of Henry VIII were found in the foundations when these were cleared in 1818. Why the Yardes suddenly sold their old family property has always been a mystery, and they died out soon after. An alternative explanation for the ghost is that he is Gilbert, a twin brother of the man killed out riding, who is unaccounted for after the age of twenty-five. A member of the family about that period committed suicide and was buried at 'Yarde's Cross', a cross-roads near Shinner's Bridge, Totnes. So it is also possible this produced the ghost.

Whether the place ever was so haunted we do not know; there are no accounts of it, and no one seems to have seen anything out of the ordinary. Though Mrs Woolner did hear of one visitor to the house (a nervous woman who slept badly) who looked out of a window about 2 a.m. and saw a young man walk across the further lawn and disappear behind the house, near the site of the stables, but she gave no description of his clothes, and we have really no reason to suppose he was a ghost.

Mrs Woolner informs me that there is a public footpath to Ogwell which passes behind the back of Bradley and crosses the little River Lemon by a footbridge called locally 'Ghost's (or Ghosts') Bridge' for no apparent reason. She tells me further that there is a variant of the well-known Littlecote story attached to the house. A midwife sent for in conditions of great secrecy, blindfolded, etc., delivers baby for mysterious woman. Putative father seizes baby and burns it on a fire, having first dashed out its brains on the wall, causing an indelible bloodstain. Midwife taken away and years later returns in some other capacity, recognises the room and spills the beans. Mrs Woolner does not believe that this is genuine historical fact, but, in view of its similarity to the Littlecote legend, considers – and so do I – that it is a localised version of a widespread folktale promulgated by ballads and broadsheets.

Another – and less gruesome – tale in the neighbourhood attaches to the old path up the steep hill to Wolborough church. Again I am indebted to Mrs Woolner:

'An itinerant fishmonger, plying his trade around Newton Abbot, found his unsold stock of herrings was no longer marketable. He was passing along the Wolborough Church Path which runs down the steep hill from the church into the Totnes Road, and so into the town. It runs between what used to be high, unkempt hedges of coppice wood. The fish-pedlar threw his unwanted herrings over the hedge – or so he thought.

'On Sunday evening the Parson was surprised to find his congregation sadly reduced. On making enquiries as to the cause he learnt that those of his parishioners who used Church Path had been horrified to encounter the ghostly image of a man hanging from a tree beside the path, and had fled in disorder back home. He was told that nothing was visible next day.

'The sensible man went to look for himself, and found this bundle of very "high" fish caught up in the bushes, and, by unlucky chance, forming roughly the shape of a hanging corpse. And so the story of the Ghost of Wolborough Church Path turned out to be a very (phosphorescent) fishy story indeed.'

Which reminds me that an old Topsham fisherman told me, many years ago, that, as a joke, he used to plant rotten fish on a gate to scare people.

Oldstone, Blackawton

I suppose that if a film company was looking for a ruined house that seemed haunted they could not find a better example than Oldstone in the parish of Blackawton. This is in the famous area of the South Hams which was totally evacuated at a moment's notice during the last war, and used as a training ground for the troops about to invade Normandy. But so well was the secret kept and so good the reparation afterwards, that but for the memorial to the Americans who died on our own beaches in the mock assaults, one can wander in those lanes and villages without once suspecting the terrible sacrifice made by the inhabitants in those grim months. Tucked away behind Blackawton stand the ivy-clad remains of a proud Georgian mansion. The property belonged to the Cholwich family for 200 years; originally it had belonged to a Saxon, probably called Ulf; later it was given by William le Spek to the Canons of Torre who built a court house, the basis of which building is now Oldstone Farm, the oldest building on the place; somewhere in the park lie the foundations of the original manor. The present ruined house was built in the eighteenth century and in the grounds can be seen a bridge over the drive linking different parts of the garden, a shell-lined grotto, and a hermit's cave, constructed no doubt in the period when every smart country house had a hermit at the bottom of the garden.

And of course rumour gives the place a ghost, that of a supposedly murdered wife. This dates from a famous trial of 1884. At that time the property belonged to a man called Dimes. He had a daughter called Laura, who was found dead in very bizarre conditions. She had been for an early morning ride, after which she vanished. She was found in a pond in the nearby woods, standing bolt upright in the water, which just came over her head, and *her riding top-hat was still on her head*! There seemed absolutely no sign of violence (nor, come to that, were there clear signs of drowning), so the inquest passed a verdict of accidental death and there the matter would have ended, tragic as it was. But soon after it was discovered that, three weeks before her death, Laura had secretly married a shady character called Hugh Shorland. He worked in a lawyer's office in Modbury, was known to be acting in a peculiar and eccentric manner and planned to emigrate to New Zealand where his father, a doctor, lived. He secretly courted Laura despite her parents' open disapproval, and the young couple were married secretly at the Kingsbridge Registry Office on 9 April 1884. Then two days later Shorland left for New Zealand. Next he wrote a letter to his wife, which he entrusted to a friend going to Brindisi and instructed him to post it there, to reassure Laura. Yet on the very day of her death a postman saw Shorland in the neighbourhood. Shorland was quickly apprehended and put on trial. As there was no evidence of murder Shorland was acquitted. He told his friends he himself was sure that Laura had been murdered or that she had committed suicide; nothing further was done to pursue the matter.

There were vague tales that Laura's ghost was sometimes seen in the grounds and it is said that a chimney sweep working in the dining room once found himself locked in and while he was waiting to be released saw something spooky high up on the wall, dancing round. Who or what he saw is not remembered. Was it Laura – or something else, quite different?

Ten years after the trial the house was burnt down and totally gutted and no one has made any attempt to rebuild that magnificent edifice. As Professor W. G. Hoskins has put it: 'Oldstone is a dark and melancholy ruin among the chestnuts, the nettles and the elder.'

The Hole in the Path

Yealmpton is a rather remote village to the south of the A38, on a road between Totnes and Plymouth. Its main claim to notoriety rests with its association with 'Old Mother Hubbard' who lived at Kitley, where it is believed she was the housekeeper for the Bastard family. A young relative of theirs, Miss Sarah Martin, while staying with them wrote the famous little poem which was published and the only copy of the first edition which has survived is in the library there. A pretty thatched cottage in the village is vaguely thought to have been Mother Hubbard's abode after she retired. The parish church (St Bartholomew's) lies on a slope below the level of the village street and presumably rests on a very ancient foundation, since outside the west end is a Romano-British monolith inscribed 'GOREUS'. The church is the result of a devastating rebuilding operation designed by the fashionable Victorian architect, Butterfield, in 1850. Professor W. G. Hoskins calls it 'the most amazing effort in local marbles', and Sir John Betjeman adds, 'the most amazing Victorian church in Devon'. But none of this is noticeable outside, where the structure appears quite conventionally medieval; the tower, however, was only added in 1915.

To this living, in 1946, came a new vicar, the Rev. A. T. P. Byles, Ph.D., with his wife, who many years later – in 1974 – told me of a strange experience they shared. There was a doorway in the south side of the chancel which the vicar normally used. It opened on to a narrow path which led straight southwards to join the main path that

Kitley

ran round the church. Late one Saturday afternoon the vicar's wife was arranging the flowers on the high altar. The light was beginning to fail and she had almost finished and was about to clear up, when her husband came to the door to meet her. He wrote afterwards for me:

'... In the middle of the path I saw a hole, of irregular shape, about a yard in width. I thought it was a subsidence, and went into the church and told my wife about it. Coming out shortly afterwards, I found that the hole was very much larger, and asked my wife to come out and see it. We both looked into it, and I suggested lowering myself into it. However, it was of uncertain depth, and when I threw a stone it bumped against stonework which we could see, and which looked like part of a wall.

'My main concern was to prevent an accident to anyone using the path. I therefore went away to get some planks to cover the hole, which now measured about three yards across. In the village street I met Mr Knight, the local builder and undertaker, and asked him to come and see the hole. On arrival there was no sign of a hole. The path and grass verge were exactly as before, with no sign of disturbance.

Mr Knight seemed rather less puzzled than I would have expected and said: "That's all right, sir," or words to that effect. He never mentioned the incident again. We left Yealmpton for London in 1950. Although we have told the story to many people, we have never before written an account of it.'

It was not until 1974 that Dr Byles, then Chaplain of Livery Dole, wrote this down for me. I visited the village soon after and enquired whether the hole had been seen by anyone else. The story was well known and had passed into the traditions of Yealmpton, but it seemed unlikely that anyone had heard of it before Dr Byles had told of his experience. As no one had thought of excavating the spot, plainly one could not hope to get any further. It may have been quite a unique event with a significance that must for the present remain obscure.

The Weaver and the Parson

Dean Prior is a scattered village divided by the A38 road from Exeter to Plymouth. Its main claim to distinction lies in the fact that a famous poet, Robert Herrick, was the vicar in the reign of Charles I; he was ejected during the Commonwealth but reinstated at the Restoration, and died there. He was no countryman but a born man-about-town and during his first period at Dean was frankly bored to tears with country life. However, he wrote a lot of his best verse there, and missed the life when he had to return to London. Coming again to Dean, he was obviously grateful to be back and wrote charmingly of his quiet existence there.

But life at Dean Prior may not always have been so quiet. Early in the last century a curious tradition appeared in print which probably dates back to the seventeenth century. In the parish lived a well-known weaver called Thomas Knowles. His cottage was in a remote spot called Dean Combe, by the lovely little Dean Burn that ripples down through a wooded valley. He had two sons whom he brought up in his craft and who expected to inherit the business. But the old man lived on and on, no doubt saying, 'I would like to retire, but the boys are not yet old enough to take over.' By the time of Knowles' death, one of the 'boys' had already died and the other was himself elderly. Phillip, the surviving and younger son was presumably destined to carry on weaving, but he underestimated his old father. Knowles was

Dean Prior

famous and he intended to dominate the homestead, so his ghost appeared in the workroom, and there he was sitting at the loom every day, toiling as vigorously as in life. Poor Phillip was completely edged out and in despair. His father had died, but nothing would induce him to keep dead like a respectable corpse. The workshop was on the first floor of the cottage and as the family stood at the bottom of the staircase they could hear the old man rattling away all day long. So Phillip betook himself to the vicar and begged him to come and exercise his authority. The vicar came at once, merely calling for a moment at the churchyard to pick up something, and they proceeded to the cottage.

They could hear the old weaver rattling away as usual. The parson called up to him: 'Knowles! come down; this is no place for thee.'

The answer came promptly: 'I will as soon as I have worked out my quill.'

'Nay,' said the vicar, 'thou hast been long enough at thy work. Come down at once.'

So Knowles slowly descended, we can imagine in no sweet temper. As he reached the bottom step the Vicar threw a handful of churchyard earth in his face. The ghost dissolved, and in his place

Robert Herrick, Vicar of Dean Prior until 1674

was a large black hound. The parson led him out of the cottage and up the stream into the woods until they reached a deep pool. They stopped here and the vicar handed the hound a nutshell, telling him to bale out the pool with it, and not to return to the cottage until the pool was empty. So the poor dog set to work and is still at his endless task, for locals will tell you that when the Dean Burn is in spate you can hear a curious grinding noise caused by the shell scraping on the bed of the stream. So the cottage was peaceful; but Phillip appears to have died the year after, so he did not live long to enjoy his freedom and the cottage has vanished from the meadow where it stood.

Now it could be that the vicar was none other than Herrick. In after years, while Knowles had been disposed of, it was said that Herrick's own ghost had been seen around his parish, though I am sure it was a gentle wraith. He was buried in an unmarked grave. He had asked merely that a few flowers should be placed on it each week:

> 'Then shall my *Ghost* not walk about, but keepe
> Still in the coole, and silent shades of sleep.'

The Hound of the Baskervilles

Everyone knows Sir Arthur Conan Doyle's famous thriller but there has been a lot of controversy about the origin of the plot. The 'legend' on which the novel was based is not a purely Devon one, but is a composite effort with elements borrowed from several sources.

First, let me say that although there are several Black Dogs on Dartmoor there is not one that resembles 'The Hound' in character.

The story begins at Cromer in Norfolk where Doyle stayed to recuperate from an attack of enteric fever, in March 1901. Understandably he was feeling particularly low and depressed. An old friend, Fletcher Robinson, joined him and told him stories of Dartmoor which excited Doyle and inspired him to pay a visit to Fletcher's home. Now the only possible source of information so far about a sinister Black Dog must have been right there, in Cromer, where the whole wind-swept coast of East Anglia is haunted by Black Shuck who comes from the sea and appears in numerous shapes, the commonest being a huge black dog, as big as a calf or donkey. To meet him is awful, but to look into his great glowing eyes means death. I

The tomb of Richard Capel at Buckfastleigh
Brook Manor where Richard Capel lived

am sure this tradition must have reached Conan Doyle's ears pretty soon, and encouraged Fletcher Robinson to discuss Dartmoor tales.

As Robinson lived at Ipplepen, he will no doubt have mentioned nearby legends, especially one from Buckfastleigh, only about six miles away, where Richard Capel is buried outside the south porch of the church. Now about three miles up one of the long valleys that run deep into Dartmoor is Brook Manor, a charming old house. On the east side of the valley, about a mile away, is Hawson Manor, a modern house on an old foundation. In the seventeenth century, Richard Capel lived at Brook; we know practically nothing about him, except that he rebuilt part of his house (the date 1656 is carved over the door) and enjoyed a horrible reputation as a persecutor of village maidens. Having captured one, he would keep her under lock and key across the valley at Hawson, presumably to keep her away from Mrs Capel's jealous eye. So he had an unenviable reputation as a violent and powerful squire, and when he came to die in 1677 his end was unpleasant. One version says that as he lay dying whisht hounds gathered round the house, howling horribly. Another says that he was out and a pack of whisht hounds chased him across the moor till he dropped dead.

Even then the locals feared ghostly reprisals so they buried him deep with a heavy stone on his head and a solid altar tomb on top. To make doubly sure they added a square shaped house on top of his grave with an iron grill opening towards the church – I suppose on the assumption that ghosts and vampires cannot pass iron – and a strong oaken door the other side. There used to be a weather vane (brought from the manor and dated 1656) to crown the edifice, but this has been removed. There is still a feeling of fear associated with Capel. In the door is a large keyhole and, till recently, children from the village used to visit the tomb, perambulate it thirteen times and then dare each other to insert a little finger in the keyhole and see if Capel would gnaw it. I have talked to a young man who told me he used to walk round the tomb but never risked the final part of the ritual. Mr Pye, the present owner of Brook, tells me the children still come up and walk round and round. He has heard them discussing it on the bus. He also tells me that there is a local belief that Capel, minus his head, still rides up the drive from the road to Brook, followed by hounds, on a certain night early in July.

Now there was a note in *Devon and Cornwall Notes and Queries* (vol. xvii, p. 233) by 'F. Nesbitt', suggesting that Capel was the prototype of 'Black Hugo'. I think this is very probable. He adds a little more to our knowledge of the old wretch, telling us that he was the third of his name, a knight, and married Elizabeth Fowell at Ugborough 7 January 1654/5. She is recorded as 'Mrs Elizabeth Cabel' and was buried in linen 17 September 1686. They had one daughter who carried the property to the family of Fownes.

I think the following is a fair assumption: that Doyle heard about Black Shuck at Cromer, heard of Capel and his end from Fletcher Robinson, and, as we all know, borrowed the aristocratic sounding name of Baskerville from the smart young coachman, Harry, who met him at the station and drove him all over Dartmoor looking for atmosphere. Now the point that is not always noticed, is that Harry Baskerville was a descendant of the Norman family of Baskerville who actually had a dog tradition. The main line originated at Basqueville in Normandy and came over with William the Conqueror, settling at Eardisley Castle in Herefordshire, where in 1373 Richard de Baskerville was licensed to hold services in his castle. From this family, many branches led off: one took root at Clyro, just in Wales near Hay-on-Wye, where Doyle visited and saw the famous inn sign he mentions. This sign still exists, but in a dark backroom and in too frail a condition to be taken out and photographed.

Famous Baskervilles include: the printer of the eighteenth century who gave us a new typeface known by his name, and the celebrated physician to James I, 'Sir Simon the Rich', who was the son of the Exeter apothecary, Thomas, d. 1596. No one seems to know just when a branch of the family entered Devon. The present representatives believe that they possessed the manors of Heatree (in Manaton parish) and Spitchwick, and several of them sailed with Drake in the sixteenth century. However, they lost their money and came down in the world, hence their descendant was not too proud to take employment as a groom or coachman. But what stories may he have imparted to the famous author as they drove over the moor? Doyle noted the aristocratic name and asked permission to use it; thus encouraged, Harry may have added some almost-forgotten traditions, that his family crest was a wolf-hound's head, etc.

Some modern members of the family, now called Baskerville Mynors, believe in the following family tradition, others do not: 'Once upon a time an ancestor of the family was in his castle hall in

Herefordshire (perhaps Eardisley) drinking. As he had been trained to do, his black hound (an Irish wolf hound) ran in baying to announce the approach of an enemy, but his master, who seemed to have reached the fuddled-irritable stage, simply lifted his spear and ran the faithful creature through the head (hence the crest). The deed had scarcely been done when in dashed a retainer with news of the attack.

'Henceforth the death of a head of the family was announced by the baying of a hound.' So Miss Cicely Botley told me, relaying the story from old Mrs Baskerville Mynors in 1963, when they were both living in the same hotel in Tunbridge Wells. Mrs Baskerville confirmed that the family had owned property on Dartmoor till a generation or so before.

All this is rather vague, but may be related to the tradition of the Vaughan family of Hergest Court, also in Herefordshire. They also had a black dog that warned them when one of the family was going to die; I have talked to a local man who claimed to have seen the old ghost when bicycling home past the Court at night. It is in the north of the county, just by the Welsh border, and if you look at the Vaughan genealogy painted on a board in Kington church, you can see that the Vaughans and the Baskervilles intermarried at least twice, so the idea of the family black dog totem is pretty strong, and if Harry Baskerville had been told of it by his parents and mentioned it to Doyle, the idea would have appealed to him and the plot would have come together beautifully. The only weakness lies in the fact that family black dogs (there are several) do not attack members of their own families, but they do protect vulnerable people, so perhaps the Hound showed good sense!

Berry Pomeroy Castle

Devon is not very well supplied with castles. One of the few is Berry Pomeroy, between Totnes and Torquay, which should be the home of the more dismal kind of ghosts, for it is in ruins, not having been inhabited for a century. Certainly it has several ghosts which have been very fully described in numerous books during the past hundred years, the handiest being S. M. Ellis's *Ghost Stories and Legends of Berry Pomeroy Castle*. Principally, there is a legend of two sisters who

Berry Pomeroy Castle: the Wishing Tree in foreground

lived in the castle in the Middle Ages. One was crazily jealous of the other and locked her up in the dungeon, according to one account, for nineteen years till she died, supposedly of starvation, though she must have had a remarkable constitution to survive that long. . . . Another is said to have borne a child to her own father and to have killed it. It is she who appears when a death is imminent in the castle: a young doctor, tending the steward's sick wife, is said to have seen a beautiful but distraught woman with a baby while he was waiting to visit his patient whom he declared to be out of danger. However, the ghost did not agree with his diagnosis, and the poor steward's wife died.

An old friend, the late Hamlyn Parsons, wrote to me about the place in 1960:

'Do you remember seeing my red cocker spaniel, Bruno (1936–50)? I took him to Berry Castle once. He had been round most of the castle, and into the so-called dungeons in the gate-towers with me, but whenever I approached Lady Margaret's Tower, from whatever direction, he went into paroxysms of terror. Even when I carried him baby-fashion in my arms, facing away from the tower, I could not get him there. He went almost mad with fear. Not until after this did I learn from the custodian that the tower was reputed to be haunted, and that in the reign of John she had been confined there for 19(?) years by her sister/step-sister/sister-in-law – and finally murdered by her. Very many saw this doggy incident.'

At Berry you can also find its Wishing Tree, an aged beech, traditionally said to be as old as the castle, though one would suppose this to be most unlikely. In fact it has replaced the old tree which no longer stands. No beech would survive that long and one wonders how many replacements there have been? The custom was to whisper your wish against the trunk of the beech and then to walk backwards round the tree three times, and providing you kept your wish secret you would obtain it!

The White Lady of Dartington

Dartington Hall has a large collection of ghosts and ghostly happenings. There is an eye-witness account of how three people were driving home after seeing a play at Dartington, and a woman dressed in grey passed in front of their car and vanished (only two of the people in the car saw her). There is also a White Lady. The Champernowne family say that when she is seen one of the family will die shortly. The late Miss C. Elizabeth Champernowne gave me two examples she had known in her lifetime, and in 1960, the late Mr Hamlyn Parsons of Christow sent me the following incident:

'The White Lady of Dartington Hall: I have probably told you of this before. She cost at least one life. There was living in Totnes well over forty years ago a young postman called Wellington. He was a very godly, clean-living young man; in fact did some preaching, and his funeral was noteworthy for the number who attended. He lived in a house behind the Butterwalk on the parish church side near where Heath's Florist's shop now is. His father and mother ... told me the story on several occasions. He met a servant-girl by the end of the drive, and, as she seemed distressed, asked what was wrong. She,

Dartington Hall

addressing him as "Postman", told him that she had made several attempts to go back to Dartington Hall, but was overcome by sheer terror. He offered to come with her, and she accepted gratefully. They arrived safely, and he commenced his return. There was bright moonlight. He had not gone far when he saw a pale figure flitting silently along. I forget the finer details, but two details are very clear: she passed very close to him, but did not exactly follow the drive. Part of the time she was on the far side of a boundary hedge, passing through twice. He was badly shaken, never quite recovered, and died a few weeks later of "brain-fever".'

The drive is a long one, nearly a mile; it winds round the side of a steep hill which plunges down into the lovely Dart valley. There are trees on both sides. The lowest gate in the drive, close to the river, has been haunted by a headless horseman who comes through the gate, but I have no record of him being seen in living memory. The other ghosts are mainly in the house and do not seem at all frightening.

Exeter and District

Exeter and District
The Ghost of Mr Kingdon
Queen Henrietta Maria
A Haunted Church?
Fontelautus Dennis
Theo Brown's 'Shadow'
The Great Devon Mystery
The Sokespitch Barrel

Exeter and District

It always rather pleases me that Exeter is one of the localities mentioned in *Dracula*, even though the famous vampire never seems to have visited the city. He selects a respectable solicitor in the Close to act as his agent in England, which is why the young Jonathan Harker is sent out to Transylvania to represent the firm. Later he takes his beloved Mina to Exeter to hide from the Count and places her in the care of his boss, Peter Hawkins. Mina writes of 'the beautiful old house' looking out on 'the great elms' with the rooks 'cawing and cawing', and she is safe there. Dracula somehow does not rumble her hiding-place. Exeter is no place for vampires and the ghosts are gentle ones. Which is rather surprising considering some of the gruesome things that have been done there in times past, as in most old cities.

The Cathedral Close itself appears to be haunted by a monk. Now and then the local newspapers report that someone passing through late at night has seen a dark, cowled figure wandering about. Monks are seen elsewhere about the city, which is to be expected in a place that in medieval times had so many monastic establishments it was nicknamed 'Monktown'. They are even seen in quite modern houses – invading two houses in Wellington Road in 1965, and a monk whom people call 'Fred' hangs around the Cowick Barton Inn which is on monastic ground; he is even seen in broad daylight walking in nearby fields.

William Oliver Stevens (*Unbidden Guests*, 1949, p. 85) has told us of an American woman who, in the summer of 1932, stayed with some friends at the old Globe Hotel in the Close. At intervals during the night they were awakened by sounds of 'Swirling and swishing noises as of old-fashioned satin trains'.

The Taddyforde Arch

The Ghost of Mr Kingdon

In the triangular slip or 'gore' of land that slopes down from New North Road to Red Cow and St David's Station is the old house of Taddyforde, in the parish of St David's. Over most of the old garden are new houses and bungalows. All use the original entrance from New North Road through a red sandstone arch covered with ivy. It is narrow for cars, which have to emerge directly on to the busy road. In the last century the house belonged to a Mr Kingdon. In 1976, Miss Dorothy French, the daughter of a previous vicar, wrote to me, in answer to a query:

'I know the Taddyforde ghost. I saw him once. He – the body at least – was buried in the garden at his wish. My father, the Vicar, had his remains reburied in the churchyard about 1900 or so. . . . I saw him one day when calling there. I heard he appeared to a young child, who shouted for mother and, pointing to a painting on the wall, said: "That old man came and stood by my bed."'

Alas, Miss French gave no further details of the ghost, though she stated that his grave was marked by 'an elaborate memorial stone surrounded by hanging chains', but whether this was in the garden burial or the reburial in St David's churchyard is not certain. I could not find it when I searched one afternoon, but the yard is a big, crowded one and very overgrown.

However, in recent times a legend has arisen. Now it is said that Mr Kingdon dabbled in magic and that his body is buried in the arch itself, and it would be asking for some unspecified ill-luck to disturb his bones. Some residents are believed to shiver if they have to pass under him late at night.

Queen Henrietta Maria

Mr G. W. Copeland, a well-known Plymouth antiquarian and, for a short period, Honorary Secretary to the Devonshire Association, passed on this story told him by a Plymouth lady. The scene was Bamfylde House, just below Rougemont Castle: it was the seventeenth-century town house of the Bamfylde family of Poltimore. Mr Copeland's informant said that a lady was visiting the house and seated herself on an old straight-backed chair by the window. A feeling of unbearable sadness and anxiety made her eyes fill with tears, and the curator heard her say softly: 'Oh, the poor thing! the poor thing!' He followed her gaze out of the window and saw an empty street. Presently he asked her what she had seen and she explained that she had seen a woman walking past, in seventeenth-century dress and had recognised her from her portraits. It was Queen Henrietta Maria, the unhappy wife of Charles I. In 1644, when the king's fortunes were at a very low ebb, she had come to Exeter to have her baby in security. It was safely delivered, in Bedford House – a daughter: the Princess Henrietta, Charles II's beloved little sister 'Minette'. But the Queen was needed in France to raise support for the King and she had to make the agonising decision to leave her baby with faithful friends and go over to the Continent. So, no wonder she was tormented with anxiety as she wandered past Bamfylde house 300 years ago.

42   *Sir Walter Ralegh*

A Haunted Church?

Withycombe Ralegh, once a village to the east of Exmouth, is now a suburb of that town, the centre of population having shifted gradually westward from its original site a mile up the valley towards the Common. There was a tradition that St Paul visited the West Country and preached at Withycombe. There may well have been a St Paul but one doubts if it could have been the great Apostle. It was far more likely to have been the Romano-British brother of St Sidwell, St Paul Aurelianus, who has left his name in Exeter and at Staverton as well as Cornwall and Brittany (as St Pol de Leon).

When the village was clustered in the valley further east, its parish church was an ancient fifteenth-century structure first dedicated to St Michael and then by popular preference to St John-in-the-Wilderness. For hundreds of years this and the adjoining parish of East Budleigh were jointly served by one vicar. When, for whatever reason, the population gradually shifted down towards Exmouth, St John's was abandoned officially in 1778, and a new church built more centrally. Withycombe Ralegh became a separate parish in 1854 with its own incumbent. But why was the old church left to rot? A writer, in 1846, gave this reason:

'It is well known in all the country east of the River Exe, that the ancient church of St John's in the Wilderness, in the parish of Wythycombe-Rawleigh, has been long deserted by the parishioners, from the crowds of spirits and bogles which frequented that desolate building and its adjoining cemetery. The inhabitants in consequence, about a century ago, built the chapel where they now attend divine service, in a more populous district of the parish. All attempts to remove the ancient structure having failed for many years, they have long been discontinued. The dreadful disasters which befell all persons attempting a demolition, at length deterred them from such sacrilege; so the grey old tower, with its venerable but humble shrine below, still braves the elements, unrepaired indeed by mortal hand, but protected from decay by unseen artificers.'

There is no mention of the nature of the disasters or indeed the identity of the spirits and bogles which it was believed caused the abandonment of the building. And the tower, far from grey, is made of the local red sandstone. The writer of this effusion added to it this

'Gothic' tale he claimed to have heard in Germany:

Towards the end of the fifteenth century the Manor of Withycombe was held by Sir Roger de Whalingham, and the neighbouring one of Littleham by a German knight called Sir Hugh de Creveldt, Creveldt being the name of a place near Cologne. They disliked each other and quarrelled continuously, Sir Hugh calling Sir Roger 'the foul fiend of ghosts and goblins', 'the Wythycombe bogle feeder' (this a particularly painful reference to the tradition that every night the dead rose from their graves in St John's churchyard and visited the squire to demand the performance of seven musical requiems for their souls, in which the apparitions themselves would join). Many years later when the two enemies were getting old, Sir Hugh heard one night the bell of St John's toll three times – a sure sign that the lord of the Manor of Withycombe was dead, for the bell was one of those that can toll themselves on such an occasion (similarly gifted ones have been reported from Netherexe and from Alwington, near Bideford). Hence the couplet:

'The bell of Wythcombe they say
Spontaneous tells the fatal day.'

And the ghost of Sir Roger thereupon appeared in Sir Hugh's house and seemed set to haunt him and torment him to the end of his days. Luckily a sea captain arrived from Cadiz and, having anchored in the Exe, came to visit his old friend at Littleham. Upon being appraised of his host's problem, he recommended smoking him out, using a newly discovered American plant. This, of course, involved two pipes of tobacco which very successfully ousted the spook at the price of a parting curse, that all De Creveldt's descendants would be smokers. Sir Walter Ralegh, born in the parish of East Budleigh, heard of this miraculous ghost-laying and when he visited Virginia was careful to bring back a supply of the mystery weed sufficient to start a long-lived fashion. The author of this story declares that he heard it when he was visiting Creveldt in the year 1829.

It merely remains to note that St John's was restored in modern times, between 1926 and 1937 and is in use to this day with the new estates spreading out from Withycombe.

Fontelautus Dennis

In the early years of the last century Exmouth was becoming popular as a fashionable town. Large houses were springing up along Bicton Street, one of the first of them being Belmont House, occupied by the Reverend Jonas Dennis, a prebendary of the Royal Collegiate Church of St Mary in Exeter Castle, for which appointment he received an annual stipend of £2 13s 4d. This was the only church appointment he ever held, and as he boasted he had refused to marry a young lady with a fortune of £50,000, because he disapproved of her principles, we must assume he had an adequate private income; he later married Juliana Susannah Shore who brought in a mere ten pounds. Apparently they produced four daughters, and then a son, Fontelautus, who was baptised in 1824.

The holder of this appalling name appears to have suffered a long illness following a fall in which he injured his head; according to his father he became possessed, though it sounds much more like water on the brain, and died in 1826. His father wrote a little book that year on the case.

The night the child died the body was taken up to an attic room to prevent the sorrowing mother from seeing it. The door had an unglazed window open to the staircase, and the coffin lid was screwed down. During the first night, the nursemaid lying below heard Fontelautus' voice clearly for about half an hour: 'his vocal tones were particularly winning, coaxing and caressing'. His sister Maria heard him, and also his mother who was sitting in the drawing-room. This continued for several days and nights. At another time, Maria, during five minutes, saw the apparition of her brother's hand stretching out of the room-window where his body lay. These constant alarms began to convince everyone that the baby was still alive, and when Fontelautus was buried in the garden, the four sisters who had acted as bearers were convinced that they had helped to bury him alive.

During the following month, tension mounted. The cook declared that, 'sitting one night in the kitchen, she saw a headless figure enter the door from the court, and that passing through the kitchen into the pantry, it then suddenly vanished.' Due to this and the agony of mind on the part of the sister, Maria, the body was exhumed and the head was removed and dissected to confirm the cause of death. Afterwards

View of Exmouth

it was reburied, presumably in the garden again, and that seems to have settled the matter to everyone's satisfaction. But the extraordinary affair was long remembered by the neighbours, and a generation later Belmont House still had the reputation of being haunted, which is hardly surprising.

The reverend prebendary himself died elsewhere in 1846, aged 71.

Theo Brown's 'Shadow'

I have been a member of the Devon and Exeter Institution since about 1948, also a Proprietor, and, in my time a member of the Committee and even a Vice-President.

The Institution was a Regency club and library (actually a cultural forerunner of the University) offering a convenient milieu for meetings and gatherings of all kinds. For people like me the old library with its famous newspaper files going back into the eighteenth century, and its unique collection of tracts, is of inestimable value. I have always regretted not being able to spend a great deal more time in the library.

However, in the early 1970s I had cause to spend the late afternoons and early evenings there. The secretary left at 5 p.m. after asking me to lock up carefully when I left. This meant I worked on quietly, either in the gallery or the Inner Library, alone except for the caretaker who lived at the back. She was a pleasant, kindly woman with large blue eyes.

I remember once coming rather abruptly through the double doors dividing the two libraries and meeting her face to face, noticing that she stared at me in a puzzled way. We simply exchanged a few words and I continued my work. In 1974 she left us. Some months later I was talking to one of our friends there, and she said: 'Do you know you've got a ghost that follows you around?' I said 'NO! what's it like?' 'It's a little old woman in black. Mrs — (the caretaker) has often seen her with you; she told me about it before she left. She said you often came into the library just as it was getting dark, and that there was this little dark figure always behind you. At first she thought it was a child, but then she realised it was a little old woman, dressed in black. She thought perhaps it was a friend of yours.'

So I said: 'Well, I often went up into the gallery. Did it go with me?' 'No. When you went up it used to wander off into one of the bays and lose itself. As you didn't mention her she saw you weren't aware of her, so she didn't say anything.'

The Great Devon Mystery

The winter of 1854–5 was a hard one; judging by the contemporary newspapers the 'Crimean winter' was decimating our troops far from home who already had enough to endure from wounds, disease and shortages of all kinds due to lack of organisation. Here at home weather conditions caused widespread unemployment and hunger; horse-drawn supplies could not get through to the villages and old folk were known to drop dead in the streets. In the West Country soup-kitchens and other hastily organised charities offered scanty palliatives. The better-off sat by their firesides and composed furious letters to the press inveighing against the goings-on of the Puseyites who were infiltrating the Church of England, dressing their choirs in surplices and using J. M. Neale's 'popish' book of carols. All too soon their fears would appear justified, with headlines in the local press about the Devil visiting Devon in person in order to embarrass the Bishop of Exeter.

The night preceding 8 February there was a light fall of snow, followed by what in these parts we call an 'ammel frost' – i.e. a slight thaw and a very sharp frost which means that the snow becomes ice, particularly treacherous if the layer of snow is shallow as this was. The next morning when the honest Devonians looked out of their houses they were amazed to find a seemingly endless track of what looked like donkey's hoofmarks, zig-zagging across gardens and fields.

Some of the more curious followed the tracks a little way. Apparently every mark was exactly the same, and they proceeded in a dead straight line keeping the exact distance of $8\frac{1}{2}$ inches apart. What was even odder was that no obstacle made the slightest difference. The creature (whatever it was) on coming to walls simply continued the other side as though it had walked straight through. A shed would be entered at the back wall and the footsteps emerge again the other side. Houses were walked over – you could see the marks going over the roof-tops. Low bushes were walked under, and a six-inch drain pipe passed *through*.

People quickly compared notes and journalists started to try and collate the reports and rumours. The first of these was a young man, called D'Urban, aged 19, who was later to become the first Curator of the Royal Albert Memorial Museum at Exeter. He listed the places where the track was observed, starting at Totnes and travelling eastwards. They included reports from Torquay, Dawlish, Luscombe and places the other side of the Exe estuary: Woodbury, Lympstone, and Exmouth. This account was published in *The Illustrated London News* of 24 February. *Woolmer's Exeter & Plymouth Gazette*, however, had reports in their 17 February issue, naming Teignmouth, Starcross, Topsham and Littleham as well, but not mentioning Totnes. How the tracks crossed the Exe is not discussed, but as the river was thickly frozen, no doubt that presented no difficulty. The previous Sunday the Vicar of Exmouth, the Reverend George M. Musgrave, had used the occasion to warn his flock that Satan is ever ready to cross our path, though in his opinion these particular footprints were not made by the Devil but by an escaped kangaroo. However, it does not look as though many heeded his cautious words, for the paper remarks: 'The poor are full of superstition, and consider it little short of a visit from old Satan or some of his imps.' An editorial comment bewails the 'vast amount of ignorance and superstition which still lingers in the rural districts of the county', remarking that in his town some of the prints were said to be cloven,

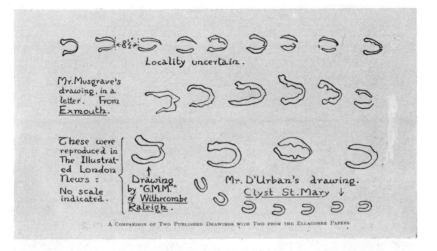

A COMPARISON OF TWO PUBLISHED DRAWINGS WITH TWO FROM THE ELLACOMBE PAPERS.

and a Dawlish correspondent wrote:

'So great was the excitement produced by the reports which got abroad that a party of tradesmen and others armed themselves with guns and bludgeons, and spent the greater part of the day in tracing the footprints. From the church-yard they proceeded to the grounds of Luscombe and Dawlish-water, and thence to Oaklands. At length, after a long and weary search, they returned as wise as they set out.'

A generation later, a Londoner who was visiting South Devon in 1855 added:

'... The track was followed up by hounds and huntsmen, and crowds of country folk, till at last, in a wood (I think it was said over Dawlish), the hounds came back baying and terrified.'

Some people even reported that the footprints they investigated showed clear evidence of claws, thus increasing the horror of the incident.

An editorial comment in the *Western Times* (24 February), discussing the 'Two-Legged Wonder', the 'Satanic Hoof' at Topsham and Exmouth, commented:

'... and some people say it is sent as a warning to the Puseyites – hence it is that the "phenomenon" has visited the Puseyite parishes

Teignmouth

of Woodbury, Topsham, and Littleham-cum-Exmouth. In this very place it has traversed the churchyard – and even to the very door of the vestibule. The "sombre perpetual" has not, it is said, exhibited a pleasant countenance since the occurrence.'

This account, appearing beneath the famous headline 'Satan in the Diocese of Henry Exeter', says that the footmarks were first seen on St Valentine's Day, but I think that the tracks were not all laid on one night but, first appearing on the night of 8 February, were found over a period of some days or even weeks.

Of course at that time – and ever since – people have discussed this mystery, and all the great naturalists have been consulted. However, it can safely be said that no one has ever propounded a solution that covers all the points. There is a vast amount of paper in journals and letters that one can consult; above all if one follows the track all the way from Exmouth to Torquay one can still find family memories, oral traditions of the event, but little solid evidence. Every kind of animal from rats to a kangaroo has been proposed. A Mr Fish at Sidmouth kept a wallaby at Knowle, Sidmouth and this having escaped was thought by some to be the answer; Professor Own offered a badger, but neither of these could have jumped a fourteen-foot wall or squeezed through a six-inch drain pipe, let alone have left clear marks on the sill of a second-storey window!

There is little evidence that the tracks started further west than Teignmouth, though an item in my grandfather's scrapbook makes one wonder. The Barton Hall estate used to extend to the coast at Watcombe till about 1848 when this portion was sold to Isambard Kingdom Brunel in order to built his great house. The quotation goes: 'On a winter's morning the men on the estates were startled at the discovery of strange footprints in the snow; the "cloven foot" was the general remark along the countryside.' My father, who often told us the old story, believed that the creature had crossed the Dart at some point and started as far west as Bolt Head. In any case the mysterious creature that hopped on one leg the best part of a hundred miles in one night was the basis for a favourite yarn.

Here opinions differed sharply. Had it one leg or two? If two they were not directly in front of each other. In fact the first point I spotted was that no one at that time and in those weather conditions could follow the tracks far enough to be certain they were continuous. Then the churchwarden of Clyst St George, the late Major A. H. Gibbs, who lived at Pitte, his family home, contacted me and most generously allowed me to consult a dossier on the mystery which was kept in the parish chest. This had been meticulously compiled by the famous church bell expert, the Reverend H. T. Ellacombe, who had been the vicar in 1855. He made careful drawings of the tracks and had found that the marks were *not* continuous, but appeared sporadically, e.g. suddenly in the middle of a field, with a flurry surrounding them, as though made by a large ice-laden bird struggling to take off. It was noticed in the Exe estuary that many of the birds seeking water were liable to become frozen into the water, as has happened in some more recent frosts this century. So birds with ice on their feet seem part of the solution, but not all.

The detailed drawings of the hoof-marks were most revealing. They varied greatly; from some sectors came hoof-marks plainly made by a pony-shoe, again some were broken and vaguely looked cloven. Some were certainly made by a stray donkey (donkeys are the only animals that plant their feet in an almost perfect single line). Some showed iced-up 'feathers' at the back, forming the supposed 'claws' that had excited a lot of people – though this meant the trail had been read backwards.

However, though we can reconstruct much of the mystery (and the

THE REV. H. T. ELLACOMBE, M.A., F.S.A.
Born, 1790; Died, 1885.

marks at Woodbury were obviously manufactured by practical jokers with a hot shoe, since they were said at the time to look like this, the shoe pressed cleanly down to the ground as if made by a hot iron), yet no one explanation will cover all the reported factors.

Other mysterious tracks are reported from all over the world, and England has its full share. About the time of our 'visitation' it was said that another track was laid from Dorset right across England into Lincolnshire; attempts have been made to link up the two, but not convincingly. Furthermore, a Dartmoor man has told me that there is a tradition of another track coming down from North Devon across Dartmoor to the southern side.

In 1955, I was talking to a group at Ipplepen and mentioned our famous mystery, and they at once told me there had been footprints seen that February at a house in the village. So I looked in. It is a very old house, said to have been a meeting house for Orange supporters. It is L-shaped and thatched. One day in February, the lady of the house saw it was snowing very heavily; she was a little anxious, as the roof timbers were none too strong, so she went out to see how thick the snow was lying. It was about four inches thick, and across the roof appeared a steady single track exactly like that made by a woman's shoe, going up to the ridge and over. She went indoors, not wishing to get wet, and to her astonishment found her two dogs, a Golden Labrador and Staffordshire Boxer, were looking frightened and refusing to enter the kitchen. After two hours the dogs relaxed and all was peace. Two other people saw the footprints. A hundred years, almost to the day. . . .

Finally, one last mystery. After I had written two papers for the Devonshire Association, and quoted the careful reports of the Reverend H. T. Ellacombe, I was told that the dear old chap had been seen in the vicarage drive. I asked, rather sceptically, how in the world he could be recognised a hundred years later and was assured that the percipient had his portrait and knew just what he looked like! I have not heard that he has been seen around since.

The Sokespitch Barrel

Some years ago I was giving a lecture on family traditions – banshees, eccentric heirlooms, etc., and a member of my audience observed that only 'upper class' families maintained such things. This is only true to the extent that in the absence of a sustained line of inheritance attached to landed property, few families of any degree bother to record their genealogies and traditions. Actually quite obscure families inherit death warnings, but they seldom keep any written record or even photographs beyond one or two generations to offer any proof of continuity. An old farm-worker friend of mine is greatly proud that I have been able to confirm his family tradition, nearly 400 years old, that an ancestor of his was killed by a cannon-shot beside Drake.

Near Topsham is a farm called Marsh Barton. It was granted to a man called Sukespic, apparently a local wine-merchant, between 1170 and 1180, and his descendants held the same farm in unbroken succession until 1803 when they sold up – a length of tenure that cannot be equalled by any other family in Devon. In all that time the acreage of the land scarcely varied in the least, though some of the family occasionally occupied other land around Exeter, and some were merchants. The Sokespitches (there are numerous ways of spelling it) had elected in the first instance to live on a saltmarsh, but above the salt line the alluvial soil of the Clyst estuary enabled them to create a singularly fertile estate that gradually eroded their enterprise. They did the minimum of labour on their land and spent most of their time hunting or shooting. It was said they could almost sit indoors and shoot wild duck from their windows. So it could hardly be expected they had the necessary energy to achieve fame or notoriety in public life. Yet they had great ideas about themselves, encouraged by historians who commented with admiration on their antiquity. Their name sounding Saxon, they appear to have been living on their land before the Conquest. Some claimed an ancestor from *c.* AD 500; the head of the family in the seventeenth century idiotically explained the origin of the name as recording that 'Cyrus, King of Prussia, discovered their ancestor in a wood, *sucking a bitch*' (thus Sokespitch)! So the silly old patriarch reckoned his family was senior to the Courtenays of Norman origin, living at Powderham the other side of the Exe estuary, loftily deeming them to be newcomers and outsiders!

But their real claim to distinction lay in their precious heirloom: a magic beer-barrel which they kept in their cellar; this continued to flow for many years without replenishment. So well known was this legend that it was a common saying in the Topsham neighbourhood of any longstanding affair that 'it was going on like Sokespitch's can'. Eventually this extraordinary phenomenon ended. A curious maidservant was sent down to the cellar to draw some beer and she dared to remove the bung to have a peep. All she saw was cobwebs – but the beer ceased to flow, it was believed, because the pixies were offended. . . . Slowly the family fortunes failed and the farm was sold.

East Devon

The Sampford Peverell Ghost
A Ghost Scare in Plymtree
The Witch of Membury
The Bleeding Hawk of Hillersdon

The Sampford Peverell Ghost

This was, in its time, the most celebrated haunting in Devon. Whether there really was a ghost causing the trouble has never been satisfactorily established. All we do know for certain is that over a period of about three years a house in Sampford Peverell was severely afflicted with poltergeist activity which seems to have been quite genuine. Poltergeists are reported fairly frequently even on council house estates (sometimes they make a welcome excuse to request rehousing), and the activity usually occurs in families which include an adolescent boy or girl, or someone emotionally disturbed. That being the case, one cannot help asking why departed spirits may not sometimes be as emotionally disturbed as living youngsters. Phenomena are very varied, ranging from the earlier belief that children sometimes vomited pins or stuck to the ceiling, to the modern throwing around of stones and coal, things dropping off shelves or electric switches turning on and off.

The house in Sampford Peverell was owned by a Mr Talley who let it to sundry tenants. One was a Mr Bellamy who indulged in smuggling activities and dug a deep hole under the floor of his main sitting-room to hide his booty. After he vacated the house, it was left empty for a while. During this time an apprentice boy lodging next door was terrified by the apparition of a woman, but that is all we ever hear of her. In July 1809, the house was let to a Mr John Chave and his wife and brother-in-law, aged about twenty. The family of Chave lived round about the area, and the tenant had a large shop in the village where he ran the business of a huckster; he also belonged to a troop of yeomen cavalry in which he was a sergeant. The household included two maidservants, one an elderly woman, the other, Sally Case, a girl of thirteen or perhaps a little older. The apprentice boy seems to have lived with them, for he was frightened of sleeping alone and a kindly cooper, who used the shed for his trade, slept with him some nights.

In April, 1810, strange noises were heard by the whole family. Fearful bangings at all hours of the day and night, apparently caused by something fairly intelligent, for when anyone stamped loudly the noise would be echoed, but even louder. If someone stamped on the upper floor, the reply would come so violently that the vibration could be felt through the soles of one's shoes and the dust flew up into the eyes. This went on for about five weeks. Then the violence increased and people were hit vicious blows by something invisible. The two maidservants appear to have been joined by two other females who shared the blows and beatings, while half the village seem to have streamed in and out of the house, witnessing the various events and counting the bruises on the women. One night the servants were so terrified that the master of the house allowed them to sleep in his room with him and his wife. In the dark a large iron candlestick moved rapidly about the room, and was thrown at his head; luckily it missed him. Another night the women were allowed to have a sword in their room, and this was thrown around and then suspended in mid air pointing towards a male friend who came in, in response to the shrieks of the women. Bedcurtains were tossed about and a strong linen curtain was rent across the grain.

Numerous local tradesfolk and surgeons, all described as 'respectable', came into the house and watched the phenomena carefully. The owner, Mr Tally, spent several nights there on different occasions, in order to prove the reports false, but was terrified himself at the knockings. A parson, the Vicar of Kew and Petersham, was living in Sampford at the time, and took a keen interest in the affairs of Mr Chave's house and declared the phenomena perfectly genuine, though he could offer no explanation. So the fame of the ghost spread far beyond the parish and caught the attention of a Tiverton cleric, called Charles Caleb Colton, an enthusiastic pamphleteer, judging by the considerable list of his works held in the British Library. He visited the house, saw for himself what was going on, and immediately published a little book on the subject which contains almost all we know on the matter. This seems to have come out in August 1810; but the publicity did the author little good, for the Editor of the *Taunton Courier*, a certain Mr Marriott, seized upon the opportunity to attack Mr Colton and his evidence, and the whole affair thenceforward seems to have become a slanging match between the two men. Evidently Marriott considered Colton a credulous idiot and tried to discredit the 'Ghost', suggesting that the whole thing was a plot by Chave to buy in the house cheaply. In fact poor Chave was heartily sick of the excitement and only hoping to get out as soon as possible and find a quieter dwelling, which indeed he did eventually. Equally, the owner had done his best to prove there was nothing there, but had failed dismally.

Colton put out another tract in September, enlarging on some of his statements, and including some essential details he might have given in the first rather muddled account. From this it looks remarkably as though the teenage maid, Sally Case, may have triggered off the phenomena. No one seems to have thought of removing the young people from the house to see if this modified the poltergeist. The poor boy apprentice is nowhere named or described so one cannot judge what effect his presence may have had.

So the whole affair gradually faded from view. It was said that the noises, etc. continued for three years, then Chave left the house, which gradually deteriorated and became a baker's shop, then a store, still known in the village as 'Ghost House'. At the present time one wall survives as part of a garage. Colton was much jeered at and persecuted in Tiverton for having promoted the story, and it is recorded that he was chased up by the Parliamentarians in the annual Oakapple Day Roundhead-and-Cavalier contest which used to be held in every Devon town; 'Oliver Cromwell' caught him and threatened to duck him in his bag of greasy soot, and the wretched cleric only escaped by producing a guinea for the ruffian.

Two years later, however, he wrote yet another comment of the affair in which he declared it was still going on, though no one could guess the cause of it.

A Ghost Scare in Plymtree

In the spring of 1841, *Woolmer's Exeter & Plymouth Gazette* announced:

'Much confusion, in our hitherto quiet little village of Plymtree, has been occasioned of late by the appearance of a "ghost"! Most ancient houses are deemed "troublesome" and such has long been considered the case with Hayne House, in the above parish, about the precincts of which, after many years of absence, the ghost has once again appeared.'

Note: there is no indication as to the nature of the ghost, in what form it manifested itself, or why. And the percipient, 'a gay young shoemaker' wandering past 'the iron gates of Hayne' was no more explicit about 'the dreaded spectre'.

'A night or so after this, a certain maiden, tripping it lightly onward, saw this phantom looking on her with pale and ireful glance.'

Of course these rather unreliable witnesses did not keep these events to themselves and soon the village was aflame with wild rumours: 'Again people say within these last few nights a brave basket-maker saw some "awful form" having three fiery heads. . . . A fiery hand is sometimes seen.' But this did not quell the spirit of curiosity, and villagers of all ages hung around the gates of a Sunday evening in the hope of a visitation. Ghost-watching rapidly replaced church-going, to the embarrassment of Mr Harward, the owner.

It is alleged that in this century a daughter of the house was awakened one night to discover a ghostly child at the foot of her bed; it seems to have departed without any communication. A child hardly amounts to a 'dreaded spectre' and the house does not seem renowned for any further ghostly goings-on.

There are a few ghostly children in Devon. Estrith Mansfield in *Our Village: the History of Holcombe Rogus*, 1952, has repeated a legend that a squire, having got a local girl 'into trouble' but wishing to pursue a rich heiress, shut his poor mistress and her baby in a tower room and starved them to death. Two hundred years later, after the house had been sold to another family, it was noticed that the faint crying of a child could be heard quite frequently. The house was being restored and the porch renovated. Under the porch pavement were found the skeletons of a young woman and a child. After these were given Christian burial the crying was never again heard.

A rather similar story was told by Peter Orlando Hutchinson, in his *Historical Guide to Sidmouth*, about Court House, Sidbury, some two miles north of the town. A certain room on the first storey was said to be haunted – in what manner Hutchinson does not tell us – and when floor boards near the hearth were being renewed human bones were found: the skull had a hole in it and a tooth was splintered. But there is no mention of a child here.

F. J. Snell (*North Devon*, 1906), describing Ilfracombe and its vicinity, refers to 'the vicarage children' who had been murdered by a wicked uncle for their inheritance and haunted the room over the kitchen, sighing. They were seen in the middle of the last century: 'two beautiful children richly dressed standing in the sunlight'. A house in East Devon used to be troubled by the screams of a little boy being chased round the house by a wicked uncle who caught up with him and murdered him.

However, some ghostly youngsters seem perfectly happy, like those at a place now a guest house near Exeter, where children are seen at night in a pool of ghostly light, playing in the courtyard, chasing each other and calling: 'You can't catch me!'

The Witch of Membury

In the records of the Devonshire Association are many accounts of witches, black, white or 'grey'; most of these accusations got no further than the magistrates' courts, for Devon took their witches as a perennial nuisance but not often worthy of extreme measures by the authorities. After it ceased to be a capital offence, in 1735, witchcraft became a private matter to be dealt with by the supposed victims, who either 'scratched' the witch above the heart – i.e. on head or arms, in which case the witch sued her attacker for malicious wounding (a farmer was sent to prison for a month as late as 1923 at Cullompton for this reason) – or a white witch was consulted to counter her power. The country people complained bitterly that the witch now had them both ways and no magistrate would support them when they tried to cope.

In the early part of the last century there was a remarkable case at Membury, a remote East Devon village near Axminster. Here there was a prosperous farmer, living with his wife, children and brother. The brother was said to be a cheerful, open-handed sort of chap, friendly to all. Not far away, on farm land, lived an old woman in her cottage. Her name was Hannah Henley (or Anley); she had three cats of various colours, and her cottage was conspicuously neat and clean. It was alleged that she frequently transformed herself into the shape of a hare and the local harriers used to chase her. As she was so near the farm, she was frequently calling there and asking for food. Everyone was frightened of her, except the farmer's brother and a young servant maid, then aged about eleven, who described the whole affair in 1882. She used to feed the old woman and the brother used to give her money and was particularly kind. But there was no doubt that they found her an embarrassing nuisance for she was always cadging for corn, bread, flour, milk, beer and money. One day he refused her money. She said grimly: 'You'll not live long to use it yourself.' Within three weeks he was taken ill and died in great agony. Hardly surprisingly, this made Hannah even more unpopular with the family, and the farmer's wife refused to give her anything more at all.

Soon after the death of the farmer's brother the youngest child was out walking with the maid when they came across the old witch. The child was playing with a walnut and offered it to Hannah, but the maid would not allow this; Hannah drew a cross within a circle on the ground. The child was at once taken ill – he would turn round and round, a common symptom of bewitchment – and died in four days.

Hannah now seems to have started a reign of terror for the wretched farmer. She drew a circle with two sticks in front of a team of horses. They stepped into it – and died. She cursed the cows: they went blind and mad. She stood on a hedge and merely looked at some lambs in the field; they all turned head over heels without ceasing till they died. The dairy was affected and the bread would not rise. One day she called when the farmer's wife was in the pantry. She refused to come out and see her; so Hannah announced she would not be able to come out when she wanted, and so it proved. The mistress was stuck. The farmer came in and heard what was going on, so in a fury he snatched up his gun and chased the witch out of the house, meaning to shoot her, but found himself unable to pull the trigger. Another day she begged barley of one of the menservants. He refused her and that night eight horses were taken ill; two had to be shot at once and four died a few days later. Next the sheep were attacked and were taken with some uncertain disease which killed them – eight or ten a day. The farmer soon found he was facing complete ruin; being desperate he went over to Chard in Somerset to consult the White Witch there. This gentleman came back to the farm and stayed there to deal with the case. Every day he circumambulated the farmstead; by night he consulted his book. He said Hannah Henley was the hardest case he had tackled. He filled an iron crock with water and barley which he kept boiling. He hung six bullocks' hearts in the fireplace, two in the centre stuck with pins, the other four with new nails. As the hearts disintegrated the witch came to the house begging for food and looking very pathetic and ill; if they had given in, all his work would have been wasted and her power stronger than ever – so he said. However, they held out and she gave up. The grateful farmer paid £100 to the man from Chard.

It is nowhere stated when exactly all this took place. The only date we have is that of her mysterious death in April 1841, and this was the cause of two inquests held at Axminster and reported fully in the press of the time. She had been failing for some while and living alone on an allowance of two shillings a week plus a loaf of bread, out of which princely income she was known to have paid sixpence for rent and another sixpence for snuff. The last day she was seen was Tuesday of Holy Week, when the local foxhounds were out and the huntsmen observed her struggling to lift a bundle of sticks over a gate. She asked for assistance but no one wanted to help her because they were nervous of her as she was thought to be a witch. On Maundy Thursday some kindly local women were at her cottage as she was obviously dying, but as night drew on she advised them to leave her alone because she said her going would be a hard one. Next morning (Good Friday) they returned and found her dead outside the cottage. The story was that she was found dangling on the branch of a very high tree which had to be cut down to get at her. But the inquest report shows that she was lying in the stream outside the cottage, with a kettle that she had been trying to fill. As the stream formed the boundary between two parishes, both local authorities refused to deal with the matter and it was two days before the coroner was sent for. Meanwhile, crowds of villagers swarmed round the poor corpse; it was said that loud voices had been heard coming from the cottage the night of the death. However, the medical evidence showed that she suffered from inflammation of the brain which was likely to have produced hallucinations and delirium. She had actually died of apoplexy, the result of her imagined struggles with the Devil. So she was buried in an unmarked grave in the churchyard.

But local rumours supplied the hope of a violent end: the Devil had collected her, dragging her body through the window and flinging it to the top of the tall tree nearby. She was buried by a crossroads which horses feared to pass. . . .

Poor old woman – she was over eighty years of age. I cannot identify her in the Births or Marriage Parish Registers. I have visited Membury, talked to locals about the case, and looked for her cottage. At the time the villagers searched her home. By the bedside they found three boxes. One contained food and money, the other two housed several toads of various sizes. They tried to catch the three cats but failed. So they burnt the place down and the cats went away. The children of the village know the witch's grave – they have pointed it out to me. The case is well remembered, but all they could tell me further was that Hannah was able to blight weed in a field; it seems a pity this useful gift was not utilised by the farmer. The stones of the cottage have all been removed and the site is concealed by a vast thicket of brambles. All that remains of this pathetic little home now are a few decayed apple trees on the slope down to the stream.

The Bleeding Hawk of Hillersdon

Hillersdon is a large house a short distance from Cullompton. Earlier this century it belonged to a strange eccentric, Mr W. J. A. Grant, who had been a well-known explorer in many parts of the world. One place, Cape Grant in Franz Joseph Land in Antarctica, is named after him, and at some stage of his travels he and his companions were reduced to cannibalism to save their lives when their ship was caught in an ice floe. In retirement at Hillersdon he was overtaken by a very painful illness which he had to endure for many years. He thought – and hoped – that death was coming soon to relieve his misery, so he organised a dance in Exeter to which he invited everybody he knew as a farewell gesture: the Swan Dance it was called. But it was several years yet before he died, in 1935 at the age of 84, and the property went to his nearest relatives.

Among his possessions was the famous Bleeding Hawk which he had been given in Egypt in 1884. This was a perfectly ordinary hawk but mummified and said to have been found in the tomb of Tutankhamen's sister. It had been unwrapped from its linen wrappings. Just before the Boer War it started to ooze a reddish fluid popularly thought to be blood, but it became quite dry just before peace was declared and stayed so until 1914 when renewed bleeding preceded the outbreak of the Great War. Lord Baden-Powell was among visitors who confirmed this peculiar quality and a friend of mine, who as a child was taken to see Mr Grant, has told me that the bird was then kept under a glass cover on the dining-room table with a piece of blotting paper under it so that they could watch it dripping during lunch!

In 1939 Hillersdon was requisitioned by the Government and the furniture, including the hawk, was put into store. Consequently no one knows whether the bird did anything to maintain its reputation.

'The Bleeding Hawk'

It is now back in the house, coffined in a casket made from wood believed to have been taken from Cullompton church, probably at the period of the Reformation.

It is a perfectly ordinary-looking hawk, with a head like the one we associate with Horus. The body looks a dark reddish brown, shiny with resins, and the feathers are getting decidedly threadbare. Mr Robin Grant-Sturgess, the present owner of Hillersdon and the hawk, has recently told me a curious anecdote. His father and mother were having a somewhat prolonged party one night. A certain Scottish guest, who had presumably drunk too much, made himself objectionable to the lady of the house, so Mr Grant-Sturgess in exasperation went and fetched the hawk. Holding it up he cursed anyone of the name of the offensive guest. This had a dampening effect on the party. Nothing whatever happened to the guest, but a kinsman of his, a world-famous sportsman, was killed the very next day! The bird had evidently cursed the wrong person.

The only other belief connected with the hawk is that it is supposed not to like women, but I do not know what form this dislike takes. It lies peacefully in its casket, in a bed of cotton wool lightly stained with red, and it has quite graciously allowed me to photograph it on two occasions.

North Devon

The White Bird of the Oxenhams
Eight Hundred Years After the Murder
The Bathe Pool
A Story of Something . . .
The Demon of Spraiton
The White Hart Hotel

The White Bird of the Oxenhams

In 1641 a tract entitled *A True Relation of an Apparition* appeared about one of the strangest family traditions in Devon. The scene of the events is a remote farm in the parish of Zeal Monachorum in North Devon, where James Oxenham lived with his large family. In 1635, the eldest son, John, aged about twenty-two, very tall ('being in height of body sixe foote and an halfe'), very pious and very promising, fell sick and died, 'to whom two dayes before hee yeelded up his soule to God, there appeared the likenesse of a bird with a white breast, hovering over him.' Two good witnesses who were present stated this to the vicar and afterwards to the bishop of the diocese. Two days later Thomazine, the wife of his brother James, died after a similar visitation. Her sister Rebeccah, aged eight, died two days after, having seen the bird hovering over her. This was immediately followed by the death of the baby of young James and Thomazine, in her cradle. Four members of the family died and those about them witnessed the bird, whereas four others sickened and recovered and had not received the attentions of the bird. It was remembered that 'the said bird appeared to Grace, the Grandmother of the said John, over her death-bed . . . in the yeare of our Redemption, 1618.'

That is the earliest occasion we can be certain of: the incident in Kingsley's *Westward Ho!* where the white bird appears to the Elizabethan John Oxenham at Nombre de Dios in 1572 has no historical foundation, nor, so far as I know, has the pseudo-Gothic ballad on the subject which was found in a commonplace book discovered at Oxenham Manor in South Zeal. This house was the family seat, but at the time of the occurrences told here the family were not living there. The Stuart historian Thomas Westcote, who lived nearby, made no mention of the tradition in his book so one is inclined to discredit the earlier fictions. They could have been based on genuine family traditions, but we have no grounds for claiming it. But the seventeenth-century events became famous. James Howell in his *Familiar Letters* (1645) stated that in 1632 he visited a lapidary's shop in Fleet Street and there saw a memorial tablet being engraved and destined for a church near Exeter. On it was recounted the appearance of the bird before four Oxenham deaths. However, the names are different from those in the tract, and the date three years

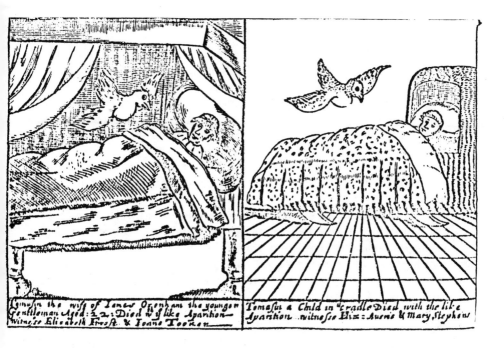

earlier. Possibly Howell's memory was defective, yet he seemed very positive about the date that he saw on the memorial. Could it have referred to another visitation? This seems most improbable. The marble tablet has never been seen since and it has been suggested that its delivery was delayed by the upheavals of the Civil War and it may eventually have been turned over and used for another memorial elsewhere.

Prince, in his *Worthies of Devon*, 1701, referred to the tradition, and so did Dr Plot in a letter to Dr Fell, Dean of Christ Church, Oxford, before a visit to Devon:

'I shall enquire of any strange accidents that attend corporations and families.... The Bird with a white breast that haunts the family of Oxenham near Exeter, just before the death of any of the family.'

The bird in these early references has a white breast, and a ringouzel has been mooted, but since then it appears to be white all over for there have been several reports of it right down to modern times.

In 1743, William Oxenham, aged sixty-four, saw the bird fluttering outside his bedroom window. He defiantly announced that 'he would cheat the bird', but he died just the same.

At Sidmouth, some time between 1810 and 1821, another member of the family died in a house subsequently replaced by Sidlands; the people who were in the room when he died, and knowing nothing of the legend, saw a white bird fly across the room and vanish into a drawer. In 1873, about Christmas-time, G. N. Oxenham was living in Kensington. He saw a white bird perch on a tree outside his window, and a week later as he was dying his wife and his nurse thought they heard it fluttering inside the sickroom.

Sarah Hewett, the Devon authoress, was told by an Oxenham that the bird appeared to him in 1892, and shortly afterwards his father died.

In this century the bird has continued his dismal work, though in 1969 I talked to an old lady of the clan who was very sceptical indeed. She said she did *not* believe in the tradition. She did *not* believe that her uncle saw the bird at a farm on the edge of Exmoor in 1919 when her father was dying, as the uncle was of a highly imaginative disposition. Certainly no one saw the bird when her brother died.

However, Mr J. R. W. Coxhead, the writer, tells me that he has heard of a more recent sighting, in Canada.

So what is the creature? A long-repressed family totem? or, in the first place, a projection from one of the family? This might well take the form of some bird or animal for there are many such examples in family history. Some 'fetches' appear as black dogs or white women.

Eight Hundred Years After the Murder

In 1170 St Thomas of Canterbury was murdered in his Cathedral by four knights who were inspired to commit this sacrilege by some hasty words of Henry II when in a towering Plantagenet temper. All these four murderers had property in the west country; William de Tracy was a Devon man who had the manor of Woolacombe in the extreme north. After the murder he fled to Exeter to seek absolution from the Bishop, Bartholomew Iscanus, and then because of the danger of the king's fury turning on him, he went into hiding. He fled to his cousin at Bovey Tracy and is said to have hidden in a cave under Bottor Rock in the parish of Hennock; later he hid in a cave in the cliff over Crewkherne Cove, Ilfracombe, on the land of another kinsman, and his daughter lowered food to him on a rope. Actually the king took the blame for the incident on his own shoulders and did public penance at Canterbury Cathedral and none of the four knights were indicted or punished for the killing, which seems unfair. Becket had made many enemies, both as a layman and as Archbishop. It is a local tradition in Devon that he had seduced Tracy's wife, before their marriage, and that the king's hasty and ill-considered words gave William an excuse to pay off a personal score. As it was, Tracy suffered no disgrace officially, and later – in 1173 – was appointed Steward of Brittany.

Meanwhile the desecrated Canterbury Cathedral was re-hallowed by the Bishop of Exeter, and the dead Archbishop began to perform miracles and was hailed as a saint by the common people. In 1173 he was canonised by the Pope and his shrine became the most important one in Christendom. But in that same year Tracy died at Cosenza in Sicily while he was making a pilgrimage to the Holy Land. As a part of his penance, he undertook to rebuild a number of Devon churches and no doubt his family carried out most of these projects for him, as they all bear the secondary dedication of 'St Thomas of Canterbury'.

One of these is Lapford church, on a hillside just off the Exeter–Barnstaple road. The patronal festival does not take place on the anniversary of the murder (29 December) but on 7 July, the date on which the saint's body was taken from its first resting place in the Cathedral crypt and placed behind the High Altar. Miss Nellie Drake in her delightful *A North Devon Village* (p. 19) shows that his memory is still green:

'. . . You have only to wander around the church at midnight on July 7th and you will see "Our Tom", as Beckett is familiarly called, ride around the church in a "hat", which presumably is a mitre, and go up through the village.

'This, I am told, is what is, or was, seen. It is true I have never seen "Our Tom" myself, but then, I have never been near the church at midnight on July 7th.'

In 1889, during repairs to the south wall, a cavity was revealed which contained a small fragment of a skull. It would seem that this was the relic of a saint (St Thomas himself?) hidden during the period when shrines were being destroyed in the sixteenth century in order to discourage the cult of saints.

William de Tracy is also remembered in North Devon. Although or perhaps because he was not officially castigated, popular opinion takes a dreary view of his fate after death. He haunts Woolacombe Sands and Braunton Burrows trying desperately to spin ropes of sand. After many years he seems to be succeeding, but then a huge black dog appears bearing in its mouth a ball of fire. This it presses against the flimsy cord and breaks it. At other times, on a stormy night, poor William takes to his horse and gallops frenziedly up and down the Sands, wailing dismally; this, as tradition has it, is always to be the fate of his family and has given rise to the saying:

'The weird of the Tracys
That have always the wind and the rain in their faces.'

Our ancestors always considered that Midsummer Day coincided with St John's Day (24 June), which of course it does not, and when the calendar was adjusted by ten days to the continental usage, certain days early in July were associated with mid-summer beliefs and customs. From this point of view it is interesting to hear that some Lapford people say that 'Our Tom' gallops through the village on a white horse on St John's Eve, making for either Nymet Rowland or Nymet Tracy.

It is strange that à Becket and Tracy occur in this area, for the Tracy family had no special connection with it, but it has been suggested recently that perhaps William hid here for a short while.

But à Becket's ghost is not the only one in Lapford. There is also the infamous Parson Jack Radford, who terrorised his parishioners with his pack of hounds, fathered innumerable illegitimate children and outwitted his bishop. One of his servant maids, when pregnant, drowned herself in the deep rectory pond and her ghost used to be seen by the villagers. Radford wanted to be buried in his chancel but this was too much. His grave is outside the chancel on the north, with a curb and a cross which is said never to stay firm. When I first saw it in 1955 it had been cemented in place two years previously, but the then Rector, Fr. Judd, showed me it was already slewing. Recently, when I visited Lapford it appeared quite steady. It was said there was a hole on the grave, the size of one's finger, that the old wretch used to emerge from at night to try and return to the old Rectory at a cockstride, but I cannot say I could ever find this hole.

The Bathe Pool

This famous pool is on the land adjoining Bathe Barton in the parish of North Tawton. It looks scooped out of a hill side, is about an acre in extent, and slopes gradually to the bottom.

The Stuart historian Thomas Westcott, writing in about 1630, said of it: '... It was commonly observed that before the death of any great prince, or any strange occurance of great importance, in the dryest time it would be so full, and continue to maintain a stream until the matter happened that it prognosticated. . . . And as I have been informed, it hath in these latter days, been seen three times in the past thirty years.'

An unidentified source dated 1817 states:

'The hollow has been examined and there seems to be no spring. It is ploughed like the rest of the field. It filled with water just before the death of Mr Pitt (Jan. 1806) and Mr Percival (1810). In 1817 it filled, and people said the king would die, and the death of the Princess Charlotte in the spring of that year, increased the belief in the prophetic nature of the spring.'

The late Reverend Harry Fulford Williams who was brought up in the parish told me: 'My grandmother, Mrs Robert Fulford of North Tawton who died in 1902, told me it filled just before the death of the Duke of Wellington, 1852.' He also understood it filled in the sping of 1910, just before the death of Edward VII, and in the spring of 1914, the year of the First World War.

In the first issue of the *Devon & Exeter Gazette* after the death of King George V, 20 January 1936, it was stated:

'Last week the pool was reported filled, and people regarded the omen as ominous [sic]. The death of King George on Monday night tended to strengthen the legend.'

When the Bathe Pool fills, a member of the Royal family was supposed to die within three months, and the *Gazette* continued:

'It is on authentic record that "Bathe Pool was out", as the phenomenon is expressed, previous to the deaths of the Prince Consort, the Duke of Clarence, Queen Victoria, and King Edward. The pool has been known to fill during harvest. On one occasion a crop of barley had been cut and stood in shocks. During the night the pool suddenly filled, and next morning the sheaves were floating.'

A folklore colleague tells me that she heard that in the winter of 1951, the pool filled steadily from November until February when King George VI died; then it emptied.

So it would seem that the Pool is still performing loyally, though not a single eye-witness account has turned up as yet. But the tradition is a very old one; we can see it dates from Stuart times, and way back in the early Middle Ages it must have been regarded as notable, for the lords of the Manor named themselves 'de Bathe' at least as early as 1281. Was the hollow behaving oddly even then? it looks rather like it. The name of the City, 'Bath' occurs as 'Hat Bathu' as early as AD 676, and also as Bade, both coming from a common Teutonic root. So could this take our Bathe back to the Dark Ages? South Tawton has a special interest for us. There is a small (apparent) clearing between two enormous areas of forest, or groups of sacred groves, known to us now only by the clusters of placenames derived from the Romano-British 'Nemet' which is found throughout Celtic Europe. In this curious gap between the two forests is a Roman encampment which is called in the *Ravenna Cosmography* 'Nemetostatio' or in some versions 'Nemetotatio'. This lies only half a mile from Bathe Barton, and a Roman road, apparently from Exeter, runs here and fades out: we have no idea where it once connected. One may imagine that the Celtic tribes retreated to the woods, and the Romans, needing to communicate with some centre further west which has not been recorded, ran this road through the opening and set up their camp to protect their people in transit. Was the ancient mysterious pool once sacred and associated with a native rallying point and therefore one of the factors which influenced the Romans' choice of site?

A Story of Something . . .

Hannah Cox O'Neill was born in 1832 and died in 1915; during her long life she had run a school, been a nurse and had written several books. She was a pioneer in education, believing that children should be taught those skills that would help them to earn a living. She lived most of her childhood at Lynmouth and took a keen interest in her locality. In her *Devonshire Idylls*, first published in 1892, she included a story so remarkable that I cannot resist giving a shortened version of it to encourage people to read it in its entirety, and demand a reprint of the book.

When she was very young, Miss O'Neill recalled there was a certain path through the wood, near her home, which she was not allowed to use because a local girl called Avice had come that way recently 'and her's not been the same maid since'. Eventually she learned that Avice, coming along the path, had met with an old woman who had an evil reputation. She tried to sell Avice a broom but the girl refused. The old one had drawn a circle round the girl with a broomstick, and the girl being high-spirited had jumped out of it to find the old woman had vanished. She ran home and from then on poltergeist activity took over. She had only to look at an object for it to skip off the shelf and, if it was cloam (earthenware), break on the floor.

One day the farmer and his wife were out, and it was getting towards evening milking time. Avice's brother takes up the story:

'"And then I see it was getting on for six o'clock, for the bullocks was lifting their heads, and the cows was moving on over the 'Little Park' towards the geät. So I follows 'em to the yard where the shippon was, and ties up the bullocks, and goes on up over the yard to call the maid to come milking. And as I go along up over the stoäns, what should I see but the milking bucket dapping down over the court; so I picked en up, and says, 'Well met,' says I, 'I were just a-coming to fetch 'ee'; and I took en down to the yard, and stood en beside of Blackberry, 'cause her were the first cow I allus milked. And then I went for the stool, and to fetch the maid. And as I went up over the stoäns this time, there was the semmet coming along, and close behind he were maister's old lanthorn, dapping along like as if they were dancing. Well, I didn't know what to make of it, but I picks 'em up and carries 'em up the step into the big kitchen, and I hung 'em up on the nails where they belonged to.

'"The maid were there, hitching up the chimney crock, and her turned round to see what I were a-doin' of, and when her faced the semmet he gave one great jump and there he was, in the middle of the floor, dapping about like mad. And the lanthorn, he wouldn't bide neither; he was off again. And the bellows banged agin' the wall. And the big dish kettle what Avice had just hitched up tipped over into the turves. And the maid, her stood there quite skeered like, and her didn't say nothing. 'Avice,' says I, 'Avice, maid, what's up, then?' For

I heard a great racketing up in the chamber overhead, where the maister's old mother lay – her that was a bed-lyer, for her were more than ninety years old. And I said, 'What's up wi' old granny, then? and what be 'em after, tumbling the things about like that?' But her made answer quite serious, 'There's nobody up there, Tom, and thee'd better ways go on to milking.' And her looked that strange there was no telling. But I couldn't go on milking and not know what was up, and maister and missus away to Ashcombe.

'"So I went to the chamber stairs, and just as I were a-taking off my mucky shoes, not to make no dirt on the planches, what should I hear but somebody coming down over the steps quite careful like, just as the little uns do! And there was old granny's armchair, that allus stood by her bedside, with the patched cushions in it, dapping down over the steps one leg at a time; and he come on quite stiddy like, and, when he got down into the kitchen, he give a great jump like, and got to where the semmet and the old lanthorn was already. And he set to, and they set to – and wherever the maid looked there was a jump; and the big bellows was amongst 'em, and the cloam rattled, and all the things in the kitchen danced just as if it were shearing-time in the big barn. But 'twas grandmother's chair that *finished* me. When I see en a-dapping down over the chamber stairs, foot and foot like a Christian, I was that terrified I runned to the stables, and I jumped on to the back of the old mare, and I rode for life's sake out against maister and missus, for I knowed they'd be on their way home by then. And, sure enough, I met 'em in the Danes. And maister, he saith, says he, 'Tom, you drive missus home, and I'll take the old mare and go after Parson Joe. Us can't stand this no longer. Maybe he'll come and say some words.' "

'And Tom stopped to draw breath, for he had gone on talking very rapid. The moon was hid under the clouds; and I think we both felt the night was rather dismal, and there was no knowing what might be about.

'"And did Parson Joe come then?"

'"Well, miss, yes – he comed; but not then. He said he must study a bit first; and he'd got what they calls a 'black book,' and he read up some 'words' in it. But, there, I won't tell 'ee what I don't know, miss. There were a many lies told up; and Avice, her never were the same maid again. And the old granny, she never spoke like no more; her that was a bed-lyer so long. And missus, her died soon after Avice went away foreign. The parson, he brought his book with un when he came; I seed that with my own eyes, for he carried it hisself, and I held his horse the whiles he went up over the stairs into the chamber. And the churchwarden, he comed likewise; and the waywarden, he brought two stoäns out of the road on Farmer Ward's Hill. There was a deal said and done. And they telled I that parson got a bit of the rope they hanged Tony Parkins the sheep-stealer with, when parson's grandfather was living to Dunster. But I never seed that, and I won't tell 'ee nothing but what I seed; though the rope might 'a come in handy to bind up the old witch's tongue with, if so be as her did have a hand in all that terrifying business. But what I knows, I knows for truth, and that's what I tell 'ee, Miss Annie. And my sister Avice, her wasn't *never* the same maid again. And the old missus, her died soon after Avice went away; and though I didn't see no more but the outside of Parson Joe's big book, I know there must 'a bin something in en, for I heard a cruel loud screech while I were standing there by the upping-stock holding his horse. And Avice, her went as white as a sheet."

'"But how about the cloam and things, Tom? Did they stop jumping about after that?"

'"Oh yes, miss. Parson Joe, he *said* them, and they couldn't do nothing afterwards. But it was grandmother's chair finished me. When I saw en dapping down over the stairs just like a Christian, I was up and off like a hare. I won't tell 'ee no lies, but that I seed with my own eyes; and a body could not stand that, could he, miss? And Avice, her never were the same maid again."'

The Demon of Spraiton

Spreyton (Spraiton) is a village to the north of Dartmoor and somewhat off the beaten track. Here, in the eighteenth century, lived the Uncle Tom Cobley of 'Widecombe Fair' renown. In the seventeenth century it was the scene of a famous ghost story which local parsons communicated excitedly to each other and to the antiquaries of the period, John Aubrey and Richard Bovet, who included it in their books. Also a rare tract was compiled from which I take this brief account. It was dated 1683, and was written in May of that year.

The story seems to be centred on a young man, Francis Fey, aged nineteen, who was a servant in the house of Philip Furze. One day the previous autumn, the young man was in one of his master's fields, when he met with an aged gentleman who looked exactly like his master's father who was dead and buried; he carried a pole in his hand as he had in his life, for killing moles. Unusually, the Spectrum (ghost) opened the conversation by telling Francis that several of his legacies were still unpaid, detailing them. The lad replied that one of the legatees had died, so the ghost requested the legacy be paid to the next of kin. He then asked that twenty shillings be taken to his sister near Totnes, and promised he would not trouble the boy further. But he then went on to complain about his second wife whom he described as 'a wicked woman' though Francis knew her and esteemed her 'a very good woman'.

So Fey saw to these various bequests, and finally rode to Totnes to see the old woman there and deliver the twenty shillings.

Now we need to remember that at that period ghosts were 'out'. Officially they did not exist, and if they were so impertinent as to ignore the teaching of church and university and appear to their relatives, they were thought either to be a hallucination, to be cured by a good blood-letting, or a demon from hell come in the guise of the deceased to mislead the living. So it is hardly surprising that the old lady at Totnes utterly refused to accept the money, saying it was sent her by the Devil. The poor young man, having come a great distance, spent the night near Totnes, and to his dismay the old Spectrum appeared to him again. Francis objected that the ghost had promised not to bother him again and he had done his best about the money. However, Furze Senior told him to go back into the town and buy a ring with the money and his sister would be sure to accept that. And so it worked out; the gentlewoman accepted the ring and the boy set off back to Spreyton – and that quietened the old Spectrum who does not appear again in the narrative.

Young Francis rode back to Spreyton, accompanied by a servant of the old lady he had visited. As they were entering the parish another ghost made its appearance. This resembled the wife of the first ghost, who had spoken so bitterly of her – and this is the first indication we have that she also was dead. Despite the good opinion the boy had had of her in life, now she manifested herself in a most unpleasant manner. She rode on the horse behind the boy and threw him off to the ground several times with a fearful crash. As they entered the yard of

Furze's house, the horse, though a feeble and decrepit animal, suddenly leapt about twenty-five feet. And the ghost showed herself to numerous members of the household during the weeks that followed, in a variety of shapes, sometimes as herself, sometimes as 'a monstrous dog, belching out fire'. Once she 'flew out of a window in the shape of a horse, carrying with it only one pane of glass and a small piece of iron'. It must have been a mighty small horse. . . .

She seems to have concentrated her malicious attacks on poor Francis. On one occasion his head was found jammed between the bedpost and the wall and it took several men to pull him out. Again she tried to strangle him with his own cravat, and she tore his peruke to fragments.

'Another time one of his shoe-strings was observed (without the assistance of any hand) to come of its own accord out of his shoe, and fling itself to the other side of the room; the other was crawling after it, but a maid espying that, with her hand drew it out, and it strangely clasp'd and curled about her hand like a living Eel or Serpent. . . .'

His gloves were cut to pieces in his pocket within a minute. Both his clothes and those of one maid in the house were damaged. Other 'fantastical Freaks' included: 'A Barrel of Salt of a considerable quantity, hath been observed to march from one room to another, without any humane assistance' and so on. When the ghost appeared as herself she was dressed exactly like her daughter-in-law. At times the young man's legs got tangled around his neck, or round the legs of chairs.

This extraordinary state of affairs, witnessed by many, seems to have continued all that winter, for it reached its zenith on Easter Eve, 1683, when one of the authors of the pamphlet was passing by the house and saw at least part of the peculiar goings-on there. As the men were returning from work in the evening, the ghost lifted Francis up by his doublet and carried him high in the air. He was missed, and about half an hour later 'he was heard Singing and whistling in a Bogg or Quagmire, where they found him in a kind of Trance. . . .

'. . . but when he returned again to himself (which was about an hour after) he solemnly protested to them, That the Daemon had carried him so high, that his Master's House seemed to him to be but as a hey-cock; and that during all that time he was in perfect sense, and prayed to Almighty God, not to suffer the Devil to destroy him, and that he was suddenly set down in that quagmire.'

Certainly one of his shoes was found one side of the house and one on the other, and his beloved peruke was high up on a tree; so this was taken to be positive proof of the story, despite the known fact that the boy had often suffered from similar seizures before, though they had never resulted in him being hurled up into the air like this. The days following he was benumbed in the parts of his body that had been stogged in the 'Bogg', so he was whisked off to Crediton to be bled. Even there things happened: a bird flew in at a window with what Francis thought was a stone in its beak, and hit him violently on the forehead. Everyone dashed in to look at the stone and found it to be a weight of brass or copper, which they broke up and distributed as souvenirs.

It is hard to comment on this old but well-described poltergeist case. The witnesses were mainly farm folk, and probably illiterate, but the account was written by a local parson and a neighbouring Justice of the Peace, both presumably men of experience and sense. What was the nature of Francis's mysterious 'bad turns'? and what was the connection between the poltergeist phenomena and the two ghosts? Remember it is stated that there were witnesses to the second apparition, though not to the first. And nowhere does anyone say what Mr Philip Furze thought of it all.

The White Hart Hotel, Okehampton

A great many inns and hotels are haunted. The White Hart at Okehampton has a ghost. It is a little boy, known to all and sundry as 'Peter'. It is said that his mother was murdered and he is always looking for her. He mainly haunts the oldest part of the hotel upstairs. On the whole he is a kindly, polite little boy who will open doors for people – sometimes. At other times he slams doors. Also he is heard, late at night, throwing glasses around, though this is not seen.

West Devon

A Haunted House in Plymouth
The Accursed Field at Stowford
Betsy Grimbal of Tavistock
Frithelstock Priory
Drake's Drum
The Haunted Rectory

A Haunted House in Plymouth

Catherine Crowe, in her *Night Side of Nature* (1848–55), an early Victorian collection of ghost stories, had a remarkable anecdote recounted by Mrs Hunn the mother of George Canning, the Prime Minister (he was born in 1770). After her third marriage she became an actress, working in the provinces. On one occasion she had an engagement at Plymouth; when she arrived she was offered lodgings at a very low rental because the house had the reputation of being haunted. She said that it would not be the first time she had had to do with a ghost and settled in peacefully with her maid and children. The house belonged to a carpenter and her bedroom was immediately above his workshop. She lit two candles and read a book for about half an hour when she became conscious of an appalling row issuing from below as of several men at work, knocking, hammering, sawing, planing, etc.

'Being a woman of considerable courage, Mrs Hunn resolved, if possible, to penetrate the mystery; so, taking off her shoes, that her approach might not be heard, with her candle in her hand, she very softly opened her door and descended the stairs, the noise continuing as loud as ever, and evidently proceeding from the workshop, till she opened the door, when instantly all was silent – all was still – not a mouse was stirring; and the tools and the wood, and everything else, lay as they had been left by the workmen when they went away. Having examined every part of the place, and satisfied herself that there was nobody there, and that nobody could get into it, Mrs Hunn ascended to her room again, beginning almost to doubt her own senses, and to question with herself whether she had really heard the noise or not, when it re-commenced and continued, without intermission, for about half an hour. She however went to bed, and the next day told nobody what had occurred, having determined to watch another night before mentioning the affair to anyone. As, however, this strange scene was acted over again, without her being able to discover the cause of it, she now mentioned the circumstance to the owner of the house and to her friend Bernard (of the Plymouth theatre who had recommended the lodging). The owner, who would believe it, agreed to watch with her, which he did. The noise began as before, and he was so horror-struck, that instead of entering the workshop, as she wished him to do, he rushed into the street. Mrs

Hunn continued to inhabit the house the whole summer, and when referring afterwards to the adventure, she observed, that use was second nature; and that she was sure if any night these ghostly carpenters had not pursued their visionary labours, she should have been quite frightened, lest they should pay her a visit up stairs.'

Mr Bernard recorded this story in his book *Retrospections of the Stage*, from which, presumably, Mrs Crowe took it.

In Celtic parts, such a phenomenon is well known and is taken to be a foresight of a coffin being made shortly. In Scotland it is called *Tathaich air ciste* – 'Frequenters for a chest' (J. G. Campbell: *Witchcraft and Second Sight in the Scottish Highlands*, 1902). While at Pont-Faen in Pembroke, a schoolmaster heard the sounds of a coffin being made in a garret over his school while he was in class. A few days later a neighbour died, and the joiners used timber stored in the garret and made the coffin on the spot. No one understood the forewarning in this case. So it is possible that this was the meaning of Mrs Hunn's odd visitation, even though she does not seem to have known of a related death.

The Accursed Field at Stowford

Lew Trenchard, where the Reverend Sabine Baring-Gould lived, has some interesting ghosts, but these have already been very exhaustively described by the famous author himself. Not very far away, on the north side of the A30, is the village of Stowford and in that parish is Hayne Manor, for many centuries the seat of the Harris family and the home of several ghosts, all of them quite quiet and pleasant entities, including, however, a headless man who walks on the terrace carrying his head under his arm when the head of the house is going to die. However, the most remarkable psychic things belong outside the domain.

I remember visiting Hayne one day in the late 1950s. By the front gate on the opposite side of the road was a wood of fairly young oaks. It did not look much more than a hundred years old. Of this plantation I subsequently heard this astonishing tale. Firstly, in the archives of the Devonshire Association, the Reverend H. Fulford Williams found a note to the effect that the plantation had once been a cultivated field. This was long before harvest machines had been invented. At some time round about 1800, the harvest was being reaped, the men using scythes and reaping hooks as usual. Two of the men fell out and quarrelled furiously. One of them lost his temper and actually threw his sharp hook at the other chap. Presumably it caught him in the neck, for it killed him. The next year, a similar incident occurred, in that very field. As might be imagined, everyone was so shocked by the double tragedy, no one would work in that field again, and it was neglected. There seemed no possibility of persuading men to cultivate it normally, so the owner planted it to oaks and left it alone.

In 1963, the then owner decided to put the field back into cultivation once more, so he organised the clearing of the young oaks, sawing up the branches for firewood. This was done with a circular saw. During the work, the saw suddenly disintegrated and a splinter hit a young man standing by and killed him. Now for the coincidence: the young man was a direct descendant of the first man who was killed.

Betsy Grimbal of Tavistock

Tavistock was once famous for its abbey, which owned vast estates and housed one of the first printing presses in England. After the Dissolution its enormous complex of buildings was gradually swallowed up in the growing market town, and the old Abbey was demolished. Part of the buildings were used in the Vicarage, and one part adjoining this still remains and is known locally as Betsy Grimbal's Tower. No one knows who Betsy Grimbal was: Mrs Bray,

'Betsy Grimbal's Tower'

the vicar's wife in the last century wrote of her:

'She is said to have been killed by a soldier in the spiral stairs of the tower flanking the old archway in our garden. Hence that tower bears her name. The stains on the wall, called her blood, used sadly to frighten me when I was a child.'

So recounted a certain Mrs Adams, a very aged resident, who had died about 1820, and this is cited in Mrs Bray's famous *Traditions of Devon*, 1837.

In 1972 I was invited to talk to a youth group from Tavistock who were spending a weekend at the Tor Royal Youth Centre. I found they took not the slightest interest in folklore, but when I turned to ghost stories, the more bloody and sensational the better – the effect was electrical. At once they started pouring out all the tales they had heard as children from their native town. Of Betsy Grimbal they assured me she appears at a window in the tower whenever there is a national disaster about to occur, and a policeman saw her a day or so before the Aberfan disaster in 1966.

The Square at Tavistock is believed to be honeycombed with underground tunnels and vaults. Normally where such a tradition attaches to ruined houses this merely refers to the old cellars, but in this case it is supposed to be the old burial ground of the Abbey. There was no solid information on the subject, but the story was told that a vicar had discovered an entrance somehow; he and another clergyman had gone down to explore the tunnels and they were able to go quite a considerable distance down one, walking freely. They came to another tunnel leading off from theirs. They paused by the fork, discussing which to follow. Suddenly, down the new way came two monks who saw the intruders, merely bowed politely and went past the two clergy, who did not seem unduly perturbed, but retreated the way they had come and saw no more of the monks, and left no description of the colour of their habits.

The boys also told me of a haunted wood outside the town. If you go into the wood, someone fires several shots at you. No one seems to have been hit. You see nobody till you leave the wood when, if you look back, you see a gamekeeper in Georgian clothes.

Frithelstock Priory

There is a whole class of phenomena in which past scenes appear superimposed on present scenery, although this may appear transformed sometimes. Do we actually see something which has been recorded as on a timeless kind of cinematography? If violent emotions, especially of fear and horror, can impress themselves on a locality this would seem to explain a lot. But sometimes the percipient appears to be involved far more intimately, as in a case I heard where a woman out for a walk encountered a party of men preparing to hang a young man on a tree. As she paused by the group, puzzled and unable to believe her eyes, the victim saw her and gazed at her imploringly as though begging her to intercede for him. She took a step forward and the whole scene, people, tethered horses and trees completely vanished. If the event she was eavesdropping on was not a pure hallucination, what was it? If it happened, had the young man really looked at a passer-by like that? As Dr Hans Dreisch, the great German scientist, who was also a President of the Society for Psychical Research, pointed out, these scenes from the past are viewed always from a definite viewpoint, as though seen through the eyes of a bystander: so who is the bystander? A lot of people would say this is an argument for reincarnation; it could be, but to me it seems more likely that the ghostly memories of a dead person may as easily enter into a living mind and force the mind to share the experience. But usually it needs a peculiarly sensitive and sympathetic man or woman to share with, and in the following story it is a small boy who was involved in a past scene, by no means horrific, but melancholy enough, and the scene is the ruined priory of Frithelstock near Great Torrington, on top of the high hills on the west side of the River Torridge.

The old priory achieved a certain notoriety in 1351, when it was reported to the Bishop of Exeter that the monks had built a chapel in the woods outside the village, which contained a strange statue and which drew congregations from surrounding parishes. All this without asking the Bishop's permission. Unfortunately, we only have the Bishop's side of the case. Evidently the prior replied that the chapel was merely a little innocent bit of piety on the part of the monks, and the statue was of Our Lady. To which the Bishop replied tartly that the chapel was of stone, and the statue didn't sound in the least like Our Lady, rather more like 'proud and disobedient Eve or unchaste Diana' and ordered the statue to be removed at once and the chapel to be demolished. It seems that this was done, and no one knows where this 'chapel' stood, though there is some reason to think that the site was subsequently occupied by an old cottage (now itself deserted and in ruins) known as Mount Pleasant, which stands on a carefully levelled area on a hilltop about a quarter of a mile south of the Priory.

Many of us have wondered what was the nature of this 'idol' which attracted people from their parish churches. The late T. C. Lethbridge considered that the Bishop was probably dead on the mark when he hinted at a dianic cult, possibly under the name of Nemetona, the mysterious Romano-Celtic goddess of the woodlands.

However, it seems that the priory returned to normal and continued its quiet and pious routine until the Reformation, when in 1536 the prior finally surrendered it to the king; the site and surrounding lands then fell into lay hands and the priory church slowly crumbled. Now all that remains are the walls and a few arches of the old priory, next to the parish church. The remains were excavated in 1932. Shortly before work was due to commence, one

Frithelstock Priory and the Parish Church

member of the committee went over the ruins with another antiquarian to plan how the excavation was to be done. She arrived with her daughter and grandson, then aged about seven. In her own words:

'Leaving the car in the road we approached the ruin down the main path to the church and followed it along the south wall to the wicket gate at the east end.

'The child, Christopher, was running ahead and got into the ruin first, and when we reached him he was standing just inside the wicket crying: "Oh, lovely! I'm glad we've come – I love this place."

'"You've never been here before," I said, "Nor has Mum. I brought you to see it."

'Christopher looked at me and said emphatically, "I *have* been here before. I have, long, long ago, when I was a very old man." Then before his mother or I could get over our astonishment, he ran to the west end of the ruin (by the east end of the church) and cried in a most moving tone: "Oh, what have they done to my tower, my lovely tower – with the steps that went windy up, where I pulled the bell?"

'He climbed a grass grown heap and looked up into the sky – "And the roof – where's that?"

'"You've never been here before, Christopher," his mother said. There was no mistaking a look of puzzlement and bewilderment in the child's face.

'I said gently, "When were you here?"

'"Long, long ago I rang the bell. It was before I went to sleep. Oh my lovely tower...."

'We watched him for a moment as he stood, and then with an entire change of manner he ran off and quite naturally began to play about among the fallen masonry in a perfectly normal small-boy way.

'"Whatever took him?" we asked one another, and I added: "None of the prints show a tower."'

And indeed a tower is the last feature one would expect to find sandwiched between the south wall of the priory and the east end of the parish church. But that was exactly what the excavators found and it is shown on the plan in the Report in the *Proceedings of the Devon Archaeological Exploration Society*, vol. ii, plate VI.

Drake's Drum

Buckland Abbey in the extreme west of the county was purchased by Sir Francis Drake in 1581. The former Cistercian monastery was virtually in ruins but the new owner, on the proceeds of his fantastic exploits, converted it into a magnificent family home. In this century it became National Trust property and is administered by Plymouth Corporation. It contains an excellent rural and folk museum, as well as a fine collection of church plate and various Drake relics and paintings. Its most treasured item is Drake's Drum. About the Abbey and Sir Francis are recorded numerous spooky incidents by Robert Hunt and Mrs Bray. Drake is supposed to have rebuilt the Abbey barn in three days with the Devil's help. Another version says that evil pixies removed the stones each night until Drake, covered in a white sheet, climbed a tree nearby and when the marauders appeared, chattering and giggling, he waved his arms and crowed like a cock so that they thought the dawn was approaching and fled.

On the main road nearby from Tavistock to Plymouth is a village called Roborough. Until the last century it was called by the curious name of Jump. On dark stormy nights Drake is said to drive through Jump in a hearse pursued by whisht hounds.

The drum was made famous by Sir Henry Newbolt's poem published first in 1895:

> 'Take my drum to England, hang et by the shore,
> Strike et when your powder's runnin' low;
> If the Dons sight Devon, I'll quit the port o' Heaven,
> An' drum them up the Channel as we drummed them long ago.'

There have been several reports of people hearing the Drum during the First World War. The Drum is heard playing itself: no one thumps it to summon Drake. In 1915 a Mrs Amphlett was working in a hospital at Honiton and she recalled many years later, in 1965, that a friend of hers had a gardener who said one morning that he had heard Drake's Drum beating quite plainly.

Drake's Drum

The Haunted Rectory

The diocese of Exeter is a huge one, covering the whole county. One of the most remote parishes in it lies almost on the Cornish border. This is Luffincott, with the little church of St James now abandoned and lying in a neglected churchyard reached through a farmyard. The Rectory has gone: all that remains are a few cob walls, overgrown with trees, a domestic pump and trough, and the upturned iron gateposts in the drive. About this ruin is a curious story.

There was a rector, the Reverend Franke Parker, who held the living for forty-five years, 1835–80. He was a bachelor and lived alone in the charming single-storey thatched house. He enlarged the Rectory and farmed his own glebe, instituting a harvest festival of his own. He also required all his servants to accompany him to church twice a day to say mattins and evensong. He had private means and was a fanatical collector of books. It is said that he lived an incredibly spartan existence in order to purchase rare old editions. The diocese of Truro owes much to his single-minded hobby, for on his death he bequeathed the whole very valuable collection of 700 volumes to the new diocese, and it now rests in the Philpotts library at Truro. Otherwise he seems to have been a somewhat despotic and possessive individual, for he was often heard to say no successor should ever take over his domain, and in his latter years suggested that he ought to be buried deep so that he should not rise again untimely. When he died he was buried east of the chancel.

However, successors there were, two who did not stay very long, and these were followed by the Reverend Thomas Ward Brown, a queer, timid man, slightly paralysed. Though the locals were rather nervous of the new vicar, the boys used to play practical jokes on him. He was a bachelor and lived alone in the Rectory. He is said to have heard strange noises at night, and one evening while he was sitting eating his lonely supper he looked up and saw Something, whereat he leapt up and fled from the house, and never entered it again. He went over to Clawton, the next parish, and lodged there. On Sundays he came over and took the services at Luffincott, bringing with him sandwiches which he ate in the church porch. There are people still living who remember him and the traditions of Parson Parker. The story is told that Brown once visited a house in the parish and started violently when he spotted a photograph on the mantelpiece, and

Inside Luffincott Church today

asked who it was. His hostess said it was a photo of Parker. 'That's the man I saw in the Rectory,' he replied. It was 1904 or thenabouts that Brown fled from the Rectory, and in 1906 he finally resigned the living. The parish was joined to Clawton.

The Rectory was left empty – with Brown's furniture, clothes, books, and even his last meal there on the table. Some people felt that if Brown had no use for his belongings it was a pity to waste them, and so the house was gradually dismantled, and being built of cob slowly disintegrated. Many curious ghost-hunters used to visit the place and wander round in the hope of seeing something.

However, in 1960 the Reverend J. G. W. Scott, who then held the Vicarage of Clawton and the Rectory of Tetcott with Luffincott, heard some remarkable traditions about the strange Parker, which he passed on to me. An old parishioner said: 'My grandmother used to say that Parson Parker was a very clever man. They used to say that he could turn himself into a lion or a snake or a wolf; and once he stopped in the middle of his sermon at Luffincott and rushed off home because he said that his maids back in the Rectory were looking at his Books, and he knew it and must go back and stop them. The tone of voice made it clear that these were not any ordinary books.'

Was it assumed that Parson Parker dabbled in the Black Art just because he collected rare old books? In which case he might well have inspired superstitious fears in the parish. Or were the boys of the village playing a cruel prank on the poor nervous Brown? Or did a ghost really appear twenty years after his death to frighten away his innocent successor?

Haunted Roads

Haunted Roads
The Hairy Hands
Jay's Grave
A Warning to Travellers

Haunted Roads

Dr Omand has discussed the problem of 'accident black spots' in his remarkable book *Experiences of a Present-Day Exorcist*, published in 1971. He mentions cases of perfectly normal, level-headed drivers experiencing an impulsive urge to drive straight into an oncoming vehicle at certain points on a road that otherwise presents no apparent hazard to safety. Dr Omand has found by long experience that exorcising the spot will often clear the evil presence that has apparently caused the trouble. Indeed he has been televised while performing the rite. We do not understand the cause, but it looks as though some action or emotion has left an imprint which reproduces a destructive impulse in sensitive people unless they are spiritually prepared and protected. The cause may well be very remote in the past. There are certain places, especially houses, which have a long history of suicides and this suggests that the initial starting point has left an emotional imprint of despair which has affected like-minded folk, and further suicides have strengthened the despairing build-up until there is a very frightful accumulation of horror which can only be dispelled by a very thorough exorcism by a priest. The demolition of the haunted place does not help much: there are numerous modern bungalows on cleared sites which continue to have nasty manifestations.

The hauntings on roads vary enormously. There is the strange man in a grey mackintosh who appears on the A38 west of Wellington at night-time, pointing a torch downwards; sometimes he asks for a lift, sometimes he just stands – and vanishes. There have been numerous reports in the press and good accounts in recent books. Not long after I came to live in Chudleigh (in 1950) I was told by a resident that a sector of the A38 appeared to be nastily haunted. There was a sharp dip in the road, and anyone coasting down this on a bicycle was liable to find himself paced by a tall figure which held its arms out horizontally and flapped. This disconcerted riders who swerved and crashed. There had been several instances of this but none I think lately. Has the tall running figure transferred its attentions to the new road? There are 'shy-points' which horses strongly object to passing. It would be valuable to plot these on a map. One such is the bridge over the River Sid, about a mile inland from Sidmouth. It is a modern bridge, though it preserves, at the side, the medieval

Beetor Cross

packhorse bridge, now used by pedestrians. I lived at the old tannery beside it for eighteen years. My old friend Mrs Michelmore used to ride by on her big black horse regularly to visit the village blacksmith. She said the horse invariably shied by the bridge, and this she attributed to the historical fact that during a skirmish here in the Civil War five Cavaliers were slain and were buried right there by the river. She supposed the horse was disturbed by their spirits.

The road from Moretonhampstead to Princetown begins to enter Dartmoor properly at Beetor Cross, marked by a granite cross found in the meadow opposite; 'Long Lane' from Hay Tor joins the road, and opposite continues down to Chagford. The crossing used to be called Watchin' Place, as it was said that highwaymen sometimes lurked here. Miss Lois Deacon, the authoress, was told that the crossroads are haunted, but there is nothing to be seen. A North Bovey woman was asked about the place 'and she looked at me searchingly and said, *"There's a man that pulls you off your horse there, isn't there?"* I looked startled, and she went on, *"You can't see the man, but he struggles with you and tries to pull you off. He did it to my grandfather once, and he had to spur the horse and pull hard, to get away."'* She (Lois Deacon) had heard of a dim tradition that there was a great battle fought here between the Britons and the Saxons – and the Celtic folk won. Another reason why Watchin' Place may be eerie is that this is where the last gibbet on Dartmoor stood, where executed criminals hung in chains.

If houses can retain memories of past scenes, there would appear to be no reason why roads and other places should not do the same. Here are two modern cases. The first occurs in a letter to the *Western Morning News* of 2 January, 1971:

'One fine morning in 1962, after filling up the car with petrol in Crapstone [on the west side of Dartmoor], I was driving down to the inn, the *Who'd Have Thought It*, in Milton Combe. The village is approached by a steep and narrow hill from the bus stop.

'At the bottom there is a sharp right-hand bend shaded by trees. I was halfway down, when suddenly I saw a horse and cart coming round the bend at the bottom. It did not strike me as strange at the time, though afterwards I realised that I had not seen such a thing since before the war. I could see the old horse's head going up and down with each step as he plodded up. "Hell," I thought, "the poor old chap will never get past. I shall have to back up the hill to that gateway on the left."

'Watching the horse and cart, I got into reverse, and was just going to back when the horse and cart emerging into the sunlight round the bend, gradually faded away.

'At the inn I told this to the landlady who served me. "Oh," said she, "that is the last of the carters. Over there by the fire is the chair he used to sit in and that is his whip hanging on the wall."'

The other tale was given me by Mr Stephen Bale when he lived at Chudleigh, and he wrote it down for me, thus (9 March 1966):

'It happened about twelve months ago last July. It was somewhere on the road between Modbury and Gara Bridge (near Dartmouth); time about 7.30 p.m. My wife and I were in a car going to Gara Bridge when we descended a slight gradient with open country in front of us. Some 200 yards ahead we could see the road take a 90° right-hand bend. We could see 100 yards or so of the road approaching this bend from the other direction. Being lovers of old cars we both saw what appeared to be an early 1920-ish Daimler Laundelette, coloured black, with a wire-netting roof rack on. This was coming towards the 90° bend and towards us. I slowed because the way was narrow, but to my astonishment, on rounding the bend the car had disappeared. There was no other turning, gateway, lay-by or possible cover for the old Daimler to have pulled out of my sight. We retraced our steps to make doubly sure but still no possible means for the car's concealment were evident. The way was too narrow for the car to have turned even giving the driver sufficient time before our arrival. It was simply a "ghost" car. We saw "it" on three or four occasions afterwards about that same place.'

No one else has reported seeing that ghost car and there seemed no apparent reason why it appeared to Mr and Mrs Bale and to them only.

The Hairy Hands

Many roads in Devon are haunted, by a phantom either visible or audible to some. Often there is a vague atmosphere of something tragic or evil which may even account for otherwise inexplicable accidents. Of all the roads those on Dartmoor must be the most obviously eery. Where there are no hedges and the low drystone walls are barely visible, it is easy on a dark misty night to become disorientated, and if the camber of the road slopes sideways, hallucinatory sensations of being pulled sideways into the ditch can feel very nasty indeed. One of these is the so-called 'Carter's Road' from Moretonhampstead to Princetown. It was called this because the first turnpike road there was constructed by a contractor called Carter; it roughly followed the line of an older road, bypassing much of the Chagford route which had been used previously. A man I knew was walking back from Chagford late one night. The lane for most of its way lay between hedges set high on the walls. Suddenly he heard a horse galloping towards him down the lane. He had no light and he could only flatten himself against the hedge and hope the horse would not hit him. There seemed to be a rider, for he could hear the squeak of harness. Then he heard the horse behind him dashing on down but realised that he had not seen anything or actually heard it passing by.

However, there is no doubt that road and the area surrounding it are haunted by something pretty resentful of modern intruders. For many years there have been unexplained incidents in which people, usually travellers, have reported seeing or feeling a pair of huge hairy hands.

My father was under the impression that the Entity (whatever it was) seemed to confine its attack to motor-cyclists on the slope on the west side of Postbridge about a hundred yards above Drift Lane where he said there was this feeling of horror. He cited two fatal accidents: in one, a man riding alone was thrown off his machine and

The road that used to be haunted by the Hairy Hands

killed. In the second case the rider was killed, but a pillion passenger escaped with serious injuries. 'He said that he saw a hairy hand touch the handle-bar of the cycle and upset it,' so my father said, but he gave no idea of the date; actually memories of the Hand seemed to extend back into horse-and-cart days.

The prison doctor at Princetown was killed on this spot in 1921. Mrs E. M. Battiscombe, the widow of his successor, wrote to me in 1961:

'The Prison doctor (Dr Helby) was asked to go to Postbridge to attend the inquest on French (who had been thrown from his trap and killed, but on another road). He had his motor bicycle and side-car and took with him two little girls for the ride. They were the daughters of the Deputy Governor. Going down the hill into Postbridge he was flung off the bicycle and his neck broken. There was no apparent damage to the machine. The children were thrown out on to the verge and shaken but not much hurt. Villagers took charge of them and saw them home.'

Mrs Battiscombe told me of another incident:

'A young man, a guest at Penlee in Postbridge, undertook to run in to Princetown on his motor bicycle to get something for his hostess. In about an hour he returned to Penlee, very white and shaken, and saying he had had a most curious experience. He said he had felt his hands gripped by two rough and hairy hands and every effort made to throw him off the machine. He had never got much beyond the clapper bridge.'

Hardly surprisingly these events were reported in the national Press, and a lively correspondence ensued, in which 'thought-forms' of vengeful prehistoric inhabitants and elementals figured. It emerged that a charabanc had also run into trouble on that spot. Laden with passengers it was driving up the hill when it suddenly left the road and dived into the ditch. Luckily no one was injured. Locals said caustically that the accidents were caused by excessive speed – 'They was goin' the hell of a lick.' Also the camber of the road left much to be desired, and roadmen were soon on the spot improving this. However, none of this accounts for the image of the Hairy Hand (or Hands) or for the very sinister feeling people have about the road. My old friend the late William Webb who wandered on the moor at all times of the night and was certainly not afraid of anything told me of an incident that occurred when he was walking towards Postbridge on this road one night. Just before he reached the place where these accidents had occurred he heard a most appalling scream. It was not that of a hare or anything else he had ever heard before. It was really dreadful, he said, and he was frightened for the first time in his life, but he never found out the cause.

My parents knew Postbridge well; they had a caravan which was trundled out to the village for a month every summer, plus tents, fuel, guests and bloodhounds. One year (I think it was 1924) my father wanted a slight change of scenery so we camped among the old ruins of the Powder Mills, a deserted gun-powder factory, about a mile west of Postbridge, and half a mile to the north of the haunted road. The weather was good and I played in the lovely clear Cherrybrook with the farm children who had a boat, or watched the fantastic caddisworms in their gritty igloos. Mother did quite a lot of sketching there. Some years later she told me she had seen the Hairy Hand herself one night when we were all in our bunks. About 1950 I persuaded her to write down her memory of this:

'It was a cold moonlit night and I was in my bunk in a caravan on a very lonely part of Dartmoor. I was at the side of the caravan facing a small window at the end, under which my husband lay deeply asleep in his bunk. I awoke suddenly with a feeling of fear and danger, and quite wide awake. I knew there was some power very seriously menacing us near, and I must act swiftly. As I at last looked up to the little window at the end of the caravan I saw something moving, and as I stared, my heart beating fast, I saw it was the fingers and palm of a very large hand with many hairs on the joints and back of it, clawing up and up to the top of the window which was a little open. I knew it wished to do harm to my husband sleeping below; I knew that the owner of the hand hated us and wished us harm, and I knew it was no ordinary human hand and that no blow or shot would have any power over it.

'I hope I am a Christian, and almost unconsciously I made the sign of the Cross and I prayed very much that we might be kept safe from harm. At once the hand slowly sank down out of sight and I knew the danger of harm had gone. I did say a thankful prayer and fell at once into a peaceful sleep.

'We stayed in that spot several weeks but I never felt the evil influence again near the caravan, but I did not feel happy in some places not far off and would not for anything have walked alone on the Moor at night or the Tor above where our caravan rested.'

This has always seemed to me a very good account and much as she always gave it verbally. We often discussed it. After that experience she thought the 'influence' began to withdraw to the northern part of the moor, frustrated by the advance of modern man and his motor cars, no doubt. Occasionally there are car accidents along that road, over a very long sector as far as Merrivale, and in newspaper reports there are often references to Hand occurrences of the twenties (and earlier) but no one seems to have seen or felt the Hands since, so I suppose the road is clear now of that particular bogey.

Ghostly hands are not common, but I heard of another in 1970 when I was talking to a Young Wives Association. One of the ladies told me that her husband was a long-distance lorry driver and his work took him down the A38 many nights. This was just before the opening of the new road, the continuation of the M5, and the nightshift drivers were chary of passing a certain spot outside Plymouth where, so gossip had it, several drivers had been startled by the sudden appearance of a hand across the windscreen for a moment. But it did not cause accidents and I have heard nothing more about it.

Otherwise I have only heard of similar manifestations very seldom; there is a very horrible, and similar case on the Trinité–Auray road in South Brittany, and a demoniacal hand occurs in two old Scottish legends. Partial, apparitions occur fairly commonly – footsteps, floating heads, and even eyes, but hands are not so frequent.

Jay's Grave

One of the best known landmarks on Dartmoor is a lonely little grave by the road that leads northwards from Swallerton Gate (by Hound Tor) to the beginning of 'Long Lane' that ends at Beetor Cross. Tourists stop by this grave and note that it is never without flowers, to which they frequently add something, be it only a twig of laurel or gorse. The grave is marked on the Ordnance Survey maps as 'Jay's Grave'.

About 1860, a road-mender working opposite, dug into a rough burial and reported finding bones. At first these were thought to be

the remains of a pony, but following careful examination they were pronounced to be the bones of a young woman, and the local squire ordered them to be reburied in their present position. The roadmender told his wife about this and she could remember being told by her mother that it was the burial of a young girl who had hanged herself at a farm in Manaton parish. Various moor-lovers have pondered on the case and endeavoured to unearth the girl's history, but there is not much to go on. A well-known writer, the late Beatrice Chase, wrote about it. The girl was called Mary Jay: she was an orphan, born in 1790, and brought up in the Newton Abbot Workhouse. She was apprenticed to a farmer at Ford Farm, Manaton according to a brief record in the Apprentices' Register which Beatrice Chase saw but is now lost. At some date she hanged herself in one of the outhouses for a reason unknown. We may guess she was pregnant, and had no means of obtaining help or sympathy in those hard days. Lois Deacon has written a poignant novel about her, based on a line from Blake's 'Holy Thursday': 'Then cherish pity, lest you drive an angel from your door.'

The lone tragedy has touched innumerable hearts, and it has also inspired quite a lot of folklore. The windswept grave is supposed to be haunted, though I have yet to hear of any first-hand sighting. Every now and then there is a rumour of some traveller seeing 'something' hovering round the grave. Gipsies were said to avoid camping on the down above the road and during petrol rationing when lorries were sent by the quickest route I heard of an Ideford driver who flatly refused to pass the grave at night and demanded to be rerouted quite a distance out of his way. When I was staying at Postbridge in 1953 I was informed by a visitor that Jay's Grave contained the body of a witch! Even her name has been confused: I have often heard it called 'Jane's Grave' and she has been called Kitty Jay by some. This was even repeated by the lady described on TV (BBC2 on 9 September 1980) as being possessed by the troubled spirit of 'Kitty Jay'.

There are quite a number of such wayside graves in Devon, normally sited at a crossroads or fork, because of the grim law which forbade the burial of suicides and criminals in consecrated ground and required them to be buried at a crossroads with a stake through their bodies. This law was not repealed until 1823. I can think of two right now: one is Green's Grave by a boundary stone between Devon and Dorset in the parish of Dalwood. Green was a man who killed himself by jumping off the roof of Old Shute House in the adjoining parish. Then there is Stephen's Cross at Sidford where a sheep-stealer was buried, the last to be hanged in Salcombe Regis parish where the 'Elephant Tree' marks the site of the old gallows.

But no one places flowers on those graves.

A Warning to Travellers

The Western Antiquary (vol. i [1882], p. 180) gives the following grim tradition:

'A Dartmoor Tragedy: There is an old ruined building on Roborough Down, not far from Maristow Lodge, of which there is a queer tale told, as follows: Ages ago, it is said, an old woman lived there, and on one occasion a man with two children arrived in a severe snow-storm. The man left the children in the woman's charge and proceeded to Plymouth, and the next day, on his return, the children were missing, and at last it was discovered she had killed and eaten them, and had been in the habit of doing so with others for a long time. What her end was I know not, but the house was eventually said to be haunted and was deserted and became a ruin. . . .'

There are, of course, numerous deserted and ruined cottages on the Moor, but I do not think cannibalism was the reason. Plague and isolation must have caused the evacuation of many places. I have certainly heard of some homesteads so haunted that they have been abandoned and allowed to fall down.

Animal Ghosts

Horses
Pigs
Lamb and Goat
Some Nasty Cats
Foxes and Hares
Black Dogs
Whisht Hounds

Horses

Ghostly horses are more often seen in association with humans, but occasionally they appear on their own. I am told by Sam Richards, the well-known folk singer, that at Ipplepen, near Newton Abbot, there is a curious tradition of a herd of white horses that sometimes dashes through the village at dead of night, rushing up on to Dartmoor to hurl themselves off a precipice. They have not been seen lately but apparently they have been *heard*.

Then there is a house at Bovey Tracy, perfectly ordinary-looking. A friend of mine was standing outside it talking to a local man who remarked that he would not live in that house for anything: there was a horse that galloped down from the Moor on certain nights, peered in at a window and whinnied horribly!

Mostly horses are ridden or driven by a human spook. There are so many spectral carriages trailing up and down lanes or drives that I have made no attempt to list them. Sometimes they are attached to local families and I know one road running outside a certain park, which the locals fear to walk along if one of the family is ailing, in case they meet such an equipage which heralds a death. Demon huntsmen are sometimes mounted, as Dewer who haunts the Dewer Stone, but I have not found one eye-witness account and they seem largely to be derived from literary sources.

However, there is a traditional horseman that rides along the road that passes the northern flank of Rippon Tor from Cold East Cross to Hemsworthy Gate. A woman who kept a riding stable told me of an odd experience she had about thirty years ago (she told me about it soon after). There was a man we all knew, a lonely bachelor (we will call him Richard, though that was not his name) with no close relations and very hard up. He loved hunting and lodged mainly with riding people, giving a hand with the horses and in return being lent mounts for a day's hunting. One evening my informant was returning home after a long day out. She was very tired and the light was failing. She was jogging along this piece of road and became aware that a horseman was travelling ahead of her. He was wearing a military-style mackintosh, just like Richard's, his silvery head showing above the upturned collar. She considered him a bore and being tired did not want to catch up with him so she kept a discreet distance between them. After a while a sudden thought struck her: he was riding a different coloured horse from the one he had been using

A ghostly horseman jogs along this road under Rippon Tor

all day. It was the coat and the silvery hair that had misled her, so she watched the stranger more closely. The road has no hedge and is completely open to the moor on each side. As they passed under Rippon and were approaching Hemsworthy Gate horse and rider vanished. He could not have swerved out of view or galloped ahead without her seeing.

Then there was a manor house owned by friends of ours. It was a Victorian building that had replaced an Elizabethan structure. Early in the last century locals said that when they passed it at night, the windows would appear all lit up and sounds of wild revelry came from the phantom party in progress. The drive was haunted by a headless horseman galloping furiously up to the house, while a scared but beautiful white rabbit scuttled out of the way. This recalled a medieval tradition to the effect that a daughter of the house let herself be persuaded to forget her crusading fiancé and marry a rich baron. During the wedding feast, the absent lover turned up, drew his sword and sliced off his rival's head. Hence the acephalous rider. But the terrified bride fled to an arbour in the grounds and stabbed herself, and now returns as a frightened rabbit.

A horse of quite another type haunts Crockern Tor in the centre of Dartmoor. The spirit of the place is Old Crockern, and he rides a skeleton horse over the clitter to supervise all activities and see that no 'improvements' destroy his wild kingdom.

Pigs

Ghostly pigs are not particularly common in Devon. Lydford Castle is supposed to be haunted by one, though I have never met anyone who has seen it, and the legend that it represents the spirit of Judge Jeffreys must be absolute nonsense, since he is not associated with any place further west than Exeter when he held his horrible round of 'Bloody Assizes' after the Monmouth Rebellion.

Miss Estelle Dunsford who lives at Ilsington, near Bovey Tracy, has heard of a black pig which haunts a bridge in the parish; it is said to have a chain trailing from its hind leg. And Mr J. R. W. Coxhead, the well-known author and expert on local lore, has told me that part of an estate near Honiton is haunted at certain times by a headless pig.

Baring-Gould recorded a local belief in his parish of Lew Trenchard that the church and churchyard were haunted by a pair of white pigs linked together by a silver chain. It was his theory that these represented the guardian spirits of animals buried under the foundations to protect the sacred precincts. It seems a bit unlikely that Christians would allow such a pagan custom, and we have no evidence that it was ever carried out in England. It may be a distorted version of the legend attached to numerous ancient churches that the founding saint was in some difficulty over the best choice of site, until, following prayer for guidance, the saint in a dream was recommended to 'follow the pigs'. This is told of St Brannoc who on waking saw a very pregnant sow before him; he followed her round until she found a sheltered, dry spot in a valley and there gave birth to her litter. No doubt the story grew up round the frequent church carvings that depict a sow and litter to indicate Mother Church nourishing her children. But the ubiquitous legend is very ancient: it is said that Rome was founded on a spot chosen by a sow and litter. It points to the very good principle that when reason fails us, simple instincts may prove a wise guide. The sow showed good sense.

Lamb and Goat

At Salcombe Regis (near Sidmouth) an old farmer used to talk a lot with a friend of mine. He could 'trace' dollies of corn and tell many tales of days gone by. One spring evening, nearing Easter, he suddenly told her, as a matter of fact, that just in the adjoining parish of Sidbury there was a pool of water on the hillside, hidden in a wood; every Easter morning at dawn a lamb would appear, dance round the pool and then vanish. Polwhele, the historian, when he was vicar of Kenton, bemoaned that people were getting so sceptical and callous they now seldom visited 'the saint's well' to look for the lamb in it. He did not, alas, specify the well and I have often wondered where it is.

Just after the last war, a hunting friend told me of an extraordinary experience she had on Dartmoor about twenty years before; twice when she was returning home alone after a day's hunting, she encountered a headless goat on a moorland road. When I asked her to enlarge on it, she wrote:

'The headless goat used to jump out of the hedge just below Sherril on the road to Babeny, and trot down the road towards the Wallabrook. I never saw it cross the Brook, but it disappeared thereabouts. I cannot give you any story of the goat or anything to account for it. But I was told of it, by someone as an odd occurrence, some time after I first saw it.

'The first time I saw it I did not see where it went, as it was after dark, and I was leading a horse with colic up and down, and when the animal jumped out of the hedge the horse reared up and pulled away, and I was rather concerned in catching him, and it wasn't until I had done so that I fully realised that it had no head, and only a bloody neck.'

Naturally she could not vouch for any of it, except that that was her honest impression. It has been rudely suggested that what forced its way through the beech hedge was one of the familiar black faced sheep, but I think it is highly unlikely; my friend is a country woman and knows a sheep from a goat perfectly well!

Some Nasty Cats

Stories of phantom cats are not common in Devon; I can only think of two witch cats but they are not important or interesting. However, there is one fantastic example which is intriguing. Prince's *Worthies of Devon* (1701–1810 ed.) cites a curious case from Izacke's *Memorials of the City of Exeter*, first edition, under Courtenay in the reign of Edward II:

'Powderham had antiently lords of the same name; in the days of K.Edw.II, 'tis storied, that John Powderham, alias Powdras, a tanner's son, gave out that himself was the true Edward, eldest son of the late K.Edw.I, and by a false nurse was changed in his cradle; and that the then K.Edw.II was a carter's son, laid in his place: but being to be hang'd for treason and forgery, he confessed he was purswaded thus to say, by the instigation of a familiar-spirit, which he had kept in his house, in the likeness of a cat, three years before; that assured him he should be King of England.'

If we may include dreams there is a sensational one recounted by Joanna Southcott, the seeress, who was born at Gittisham, near Honiton in 1750, and before she betook herself to London to form her new religious sect was employed in Exeter and East Devon. Although practically illiterate she dictated quantities of tracts and correspondence. In 1804 she recorded this memory from her younger days:

'The dream that was in my view, was of two servant maids, that lived with my Grandmother. After they were gone away, one of the maids that was very fond of my Grandmother (as well as of the other) came one day to my Grandmother and wept bitterly about a dream that she had had. She dreamt, that in Caddy-fields, between Ortrey and Fairmile, she was walking, and in Caddy-fields she met a Cat, sitting upon a gate, which scratched her upon the right breast till she bled to death. My Grandmother went to comfort her, and begged her never to go that way alone. Whether it was that night, or a few nights after, I cannot remember, but at the very same place she dreamt the Cat met her, she was found as it was supposed ravished and murdered. She was found murdered, and by the Jury judged to be ravished. The young man that had courted her left Ortrey and was never heard of afterwards; so it was supposed the deed was done by him.'

By 'Ortrey' she presumably meant Ottery St Mary. 'Caddy' must be Cadhay, about a mile west from Ottery, and Fairmile is a little way north on the main London road.

Foxes and Hares

It was commonly believed that witches could transform themselves into hares. In two places in Devon, Tavistock and Chagford, on opposite sides of Dartmoor, similar stories are found, that an old witch who possessed the gift of transvection used to capitalise on it. She would send her little grandson to the local Master of the harriers and report knowing of the whereabouts of a hare. The Master would give the child two shillings and sixpence as a reward, and set out. The witch would show herself as a hare and lead the hounds for a good run till she had had enough, when she would dart back into her cottage and change again into human shape. On one occasion the hounds were getting too close, and the grandson was heard calling: 'Run, granny, run!' and as the old woman was scrambling in through her window the foremost hound nipped her leg. When the hunt came up to the cottage they could see the witch hastily binding up her torn leg.

Almost within living memory, it was said of an old couple living at Folly Gate, between Okehampton and Hatherleigh, that they had a quarrel and the old man snatched up his gun and walked out of the cottage intending to shoot a rabbit for their dinner, hoping his wife would be in a better temper by the time he came home. While he was out he saw a hare in front of him. He considered shooting this, but decided against it. When he got home, he remarked on this, and his wife said it was a good thing he had thought better of it because she was the hare!

There is a gruesome story from the centre of Dartmoor about foxes which is worth recalling: it was told by the Reverend Hugh Breton in his *The Heart of Dartmoor*:

'Many years ago, near Longaford Tor, a native, living at Powder Mills Cottages, on passing under the tor on its E. side, after spending a pleasant evening at Postbridge, got lost in the snow, and his body was never seen again, although diligently sought for, until one day a son of Mrs Smith, of Powdermills Farm, whilst gathering in sheep, found the skull of a man lying just inside a fox's hole. This led to the further discovery of human bones near by. These were presumed to be the remains of the lost shepherd.

'The superstition of the folks near by still prevents them from passing this spot at night, for it is reported that during the week preceding Christmas phantom foxes can be seen, and their weird barking heard during the night, and nothing would persuade any local folks to venture near these so-called man-killing foxes.'

Obviously there is no proof that the foxes did kill the man. In the depth of a hard winter foxes will eat any body lying around. I once came upon half a pony chewed like this, and at quite a distance, say a hundred yards away, I came on the other half. As for the barking on the week before Christmas, this is the normal courting procedure. I heard them barking in November at Broadclyst not long ago. Nor can I see why man-eating foxes should haunt the area afterwards. I can hardly credit them with guilty consciences, but it makes a good story!

Black Dogs

One of my main interests in folklore is the problem surrounding the strange ghosts that are usually described as black dogs. I suppose the starting-point was reading *The Hound of the Baskervilles* when I was young and this was revived during the last war when I was stationed in Cornwall and encountered a local family legend attached to Harlyn Manor, near Padstow, although upon investigation I found that the ominous creature had not been seen in living memory. After I came home and started reading up Devon material I found that there are quite a number of Devon examples, and friends have added to the list. There seem to be at least fifty black dogs here. There are also some phantom dogs of different colours, white, etc. but they show no difference in character from the black ones. I have also compiled a list for the whole of the country. This runs into hundreds, and they are still coming in. They are not the same thing as the ghosts of dead pets, but appear to possess symbolic factors. Often they are said to represent deceased people, or they are seen accompanying ordinary ghosts. Some are family dogs that come to warn of an approaching loss; mostly they are attached to a definite locality such as a house, a crossroads, a bridge, or an old burial-place. Some patrol a sector of road – very often an ancient trackway. Quite often wayside inns are named The Black Dog on account of such traditional haunting, but this cannot be relied on as evidence because landlords are free to name or re-name their pubs according to their fancy.

There is a great deal of superstition clinging to these apparitions:

many folk think they are ominous and to see one will signify your death within the year. Some say that they are physically harmful or even demoniacal. A whole book by an American woman scholar was devoted to the theory that most black dogs represent the Devil. Personally I think this is an exaggeration. Dogs, ghostly and otherwise, are friendly to humans and there are numerous anecdotes of them accompanying lonely or endangered people at night-time. Here is a nice example sent to me by a professor of epidemiology:

'My mother was not free from country superstitions although she was a devotedly God-fearing woman, with a firm faith in her God and a strong belief in the efficacy of prayer. I remember, still vividly, her story of a personal experience . . . in my boyhood memories. One moonlight summer night, as a girl of sixteen or seventeen, she found herself in circumstances which necessitated a walk – if I remember rightly – from Sampford Courtenay to Okehampton. At one particular stage of the walk – which I think passed through a belt of woodland – she became very frightened for some reason that I cannot now remember, and in her fear prayed that she might have some companion to protect her. Very soon a large black dog appeared from the wood and paced quietly by her side until she was entering the outskirts of Okehampton – she lived in a lovely old house "Castle Villa", the garden of which backed on to the River Okement.'

The professor does not tell us how the dog parted from the girl; usually it is stated that the traveller looks round intending to take the dog into the house and reward it with a good meal – but it is not there. To forestall a possible theory it should be pointed out that these protectors do not confine their care to women: there are several cases where the vulnerable traveller is a man. To would-be attackers (footpads, etc.) the dog of course appears horrific – hence its commonly sinister reputation. There was supposed to be one such at a crossroads on the road down from Princetown to Roborough. It was the ghost of a dog whose master had been set upon and murdered, and the dog is still attacking any passer-by in case it is one of the thugs.

Many roads, especially on Dartmoor and across North Devon, are supposed to be haunted by these dogs. Separate sightings indicate long runs following existing roads, but ancient tracks that must be prehistoric in origin were also used. A fascinating description of these was compiled by the late Mrs Barbara Carbonell who lived in the area for most of her life. Her notes were published in

Okehampton Castle

J. Wentworth Day's *A Ghost-Hunter's Game Book* (Muller, 1958), Chapter XVII. This most enthralling chapter should be read by everyone interested in the subject. Mrs Carbonell found what looks like a system of forgotten roads right across North Devon; it is my belief that one of these lines crosses the Tamar in the Launceston direction and continues into a Cornish system discovered by Miss Barbara Spooner which ends near Liskeard. There is also a line across Dartmoor starting either near North Bovey or at Doccombe ('Dog-combe'?) east of Moretonhampstead, running westwards through Postbridge down to the lair of the Roborough dog mentioned above. In between comes the ancient Warren House Inn. Of this sector, Mr E. F. Hext of Chagford wrote in 1960:

'My story is that about 36 years ago, my father-in-law was passing the Warren House Inn about 12.30 a.m. on his pony when all of a sudden he saw this big black curly dog, running alongside him. It was black and it stood about 3 feet tall. He tried to touch it but just could not get near it. It followed him about 300 yards and then it vanished.'

At Tavistock there is the legend of Lady Howard who drives every night from the gatehouse of Fitzford, along the old road round the western borders of the moor to Okehampton Castle and back. Her coach is preceded by a black greyhound with but one eye, in the middle of its forehead. Some nights she gives the headless coachman a holiday and then she does the journey herself as a black dog. She was a real, historic character who lived in the seventeenth century, a very rich, but unpleasant person. I consider that her legend is imposed on an older tradition of a dog-haunted road.

Mrs E. G. Pearse of Sticklepath wrote to me in 1960:

'About fifty years ago I was returning home late one evening from a tea-party at a farm with my little girl on a donkey (well known as Romeo). We were taking a short cut to the furze-brake just across the river, where the donkey was always unsaddled and turned loose. As we were going down the lane by Okehampton Castle a huge Black Dog as big as a pony, jumped out of the Castle grounds and stood glaring at us. And though Romeo was always anxious to get back to his grazing ground, nothing would induce him to go on, even after the dog had disappeared. We had to make a very long detour to reach home. I think we were less frightened than Romeo, as at that time we had not heard much about Lady Howard, but we never found out whose dog it was.'

In answer to a question from me, she said she had not noticed where the dog went as she was too busy holding on to the donkey, but assumed it jumped back over the wall again. She never claimed for a moment it was a ghost, but knowing my interest told me the story exactly as it seemed to her at the time, and repeated it for the B.B.C. in a 'Tonight' interview in February 1960. However, in 1967 Mrs Pearse told me of a curious coincidence:

'A Dr L — living in Okehampton has lately become the owner of a black labrador dog and took it for a walk past the Castle gate and up the lane beside the wall of the Castle grounds. When it got half way up this lane it stopped dead with stiffened feet and hackles up, and nothing would induce it to go any further, so the man had to turn round and go home.

'This happened at exactly the same spot as where I saw a huge black dog disappear over the wall.'

In the parish of Washford Pyne there are two hamlets, Upper Black Dog and Lower Black Dog. These take their name from an inn of that name which stands on a crossroads which was once a wild open heath, though now a few houses have clustered round it. Beside the crossroads is an old well. The local tradition is that there used to be a tunnel leading from the crossroads to earthworks ('Berry Castle') nearly a mile to the south. The mythical tunnel leads from the old well, and at the time of the Civil War the entrance was guarded by the ghostly Black Dog. I heard this from a resident of the hamlet, the late Mrs Whitfield, in 1960. A few years earlier I was passing the inn and stopped to get a photo of the inn and the well. As I paused a motor cycle came dashing up from the west side, followed by an enormous black alsatian. The motor cyclist stopped, exclaiming, 'This infernal dog has been following me for miles!' and shot off on the Washford Pyne road. The dog, obviously lost, stared wildly round and eventually trotted off down another road. I quickly snapped it – and the result is the nearest I have to show of a ghostly black dog! Alas, it is all too solid.

My 'Black Dog'

Copplestone Cross, a Saxon junction where Black Dogs pass . . . . .

The Black Dog Inn at Uplyme, a mile inland from Lyme Regis, is well known. It lies on a Y-junction between the main road from Lyme to Axminster, and Hayes Lane, which was once called Dog Lane. Some little way down this is a large house called Haye where Prince Maurice set up his headquarters when he was campaigning in this neighbourhood. The Black Dog story is often claimed for Dorset as the boundary runs past the pub, but actually the building (not the original one) stands in Devon and so does the cottage where the ghost was first seen, though a villa has since replaced this.

The legend was first published in 1866 by Larwood and Hotten in their *History of Signboards* but it was repeated in *Chambers' Book of Days*, 1888, from which I summarise it.

A farmer lived in the cottage, but every night a large black dog used to seat himself in the opposite chimney corner. Gradually the farmer grew accustomed to seeing it around, despite the jeers of his friends who wanted him to chase it away. 'Why should I?' he used to reply. 'He costs me nothing – he eats nothing, he drinks nothing, he interferes with no one. He is the quietest and frugalest creature in the house.'

However, one night his patience snapped. He seized a poker and chased the dog out of the room. And either in the porch or in an attic room the dog made a sudden leap upward through the ceiling – the farmer struck up at it and made a huge hole in the plaster – and down fell a heap of coins. These were gold and silver of the reign of Charles I, and the sum was enough to enable the farmer to purchase the cottage opposite and start a wayside inn.

The dog thenceforward kept away from the farm, but took to patrolling Dog Lane. In 1856 a local woman reported seeing the dog at night-time. He passed close to her and she was aware of the air being cold and dank. She looked back at him:

'I saw him growing bigger and bigger as he went along, till he was as high as the trees by the roadside, and then seeming to swell into a large cloud, he vanished in the air. . . . My husband said he saw nothing but a vapour or cloud coming up from the sea.'

Now when I first visited the Inn many years ago and talked to the proprietors they assured me that they had not seen the dog themselves, though they had met people who thought they had, and the ghost is supposed to cross the county boundary every night, rattling chains as he goes. When I revisited the pub in 1960 I heard an astonishing story. The previous early autumn (1959) when the comings and goings of holidaymakers were still hectic, three people had arrived and booked in for the night – a youngish couple and their son, aged about ten. They had had dinner and then took themselves for a short walk in the evening down Haye Lane. At a point where the lane is enclosed by hedges on both sides, suddenly out of one hedge appeared a black dog, at about eye-level, and floated in front of them straight across the lane and into the hedge opposite. All three saw it and returned to the inn decidedly shaken. We have no reason to suppose they had heard the old story, but, of course, subconsciously they might have noted the name of the pub.

Whisht Hounds

Apart from pixies I suppose whisht hounds are the best known of spectral visions associated with Devon, especially Dartmoor. 'Whisht' is a west-country term meaning spooky, derived from 'Wisc', a name for Odin. The hounds are said to be black and the pack is sometimes led by a Dark Huntsman on foot or on horseback. It is dangerous to meet them head on – if you see them approaching you must lie flat on your face with arms and legs crossed and repeat the Lord's Prayer till they are past. For ordinary dogs to hear them baying is certain death. Numerous stories used to be current about them in the last century, but one does not hear anything of them now. In the northern part of the county they were known as 'Yeth' (Heath) hounds. On Dartmoor they were thought to emerge from Wistman's Wood every St John's Eve, when presumably people were careful to keep their dogs shut up. The Dewer Stone, a massive rock formation on Shaugh Moor overlooking the wooded gorge of the River Meavy, is the special haunt of the demon huntsman Dewer, who ranges the moor on stormy nights.

In the 1890s, the whisht hounds were heard at Okehampton. There was a big stable there, and late at night the men heard a ghostly baying of many hounds up on Meldon Hill. Although the horses were all settled for the night, they became extremely agitated and sweated profusely, and all had to be rubbed down again.

The late Miss Ursula Radford, the well-known antiquarian, told me of a woman who had actually seen the whisht hounds at Benjie (or Bench) Tor some years ago, but she could not give me any more details, which is a pity because it is the only actual sighting I have been told about.

It was believed that either the hounds were chasing up the souls of children who had not been baptised before they died, or that they were actually the transformed souls of unbaptised babies presumably chasing up their negligent parents: both equally unacceptable notions these days.

A Miscellany of Devon Ghosts

Some Throw-Backs
Phantom Houses
Reginald de Mohun
The 'Dream Church'
Pixies
Sealed Rooms – and Their Occupants
Haunted Waters
Cutty Dyer

Some Throw-Backs

Many – perhaps most – ghostly apparitions seem to throw a picture of the past on a modern background, while ignoring the present-day percipient. On Dartmoor we have occasional sightings of little dark men in skins or sacking.

Near Kilmington, in East Devon, by a turning to Shute, I have been told that Roman soldiers march away from the main road and along a disused track every Midsummer Eve, though I have yet to meet anyone who claims to have seen this remarkable sight. It is a section of the old Roman road from Dorchester to Exeter.

One day in June, about twenty years ago, a lady riding on the moor near Lustleigh saw a band of horsemen in early medieval garb; at the time she thought they might be the thirteenth-century boundary commission who had been ordered to determine the Forest bounds, but the place is some distance from the Forest of Dartmoor, so that if her idea was correct they must have been leaving the moor, having completed their work.

The late Reverend Dom John Stephan, O.S.B., of Buckfast Abbey has told us of a man he met in 1920, who as a boy had visited Buckfastleigh in 1872 or 1873 and went fishing on the River Dart. He walked up the river from Dart Bridge as far as a pool facing the old Abbey ruins. He heard a rustling of leaves behind him and when he looked round he saw a number of monks, wearing habits of either white or grey. They walked in Indian file through the bushes and vanished from sight. Now the point is that monks only returned to Buckfast in 1882, and they were Benedictines, who wear black. The only monks who wear grey, were the Savigny monks ('Grey Friars') who were at Buckfast in the early twelfth century; they were followed by Cistercians in 1148 who were 'White Monks', and, of course, none of these could have been seen at Buckfast after the Dissolution of the Monasteries in the sixteenth century.

The fearful Prayerbook Rebellion took place in 1549 when Cornishmen marched up to Exeter and were joined by the men of Devon to oppose the introduction of the Book of Common Prayer. They were horribly slaughtered by the King's army; the sympathising villages round Exeter were all fired and devastated for years after but the event has left curiously little in the way of hauntings, though the memory of those times is remarkably fresh. One of the battles took place on the Exeter to Honiton road where it crosses the River Otter at Fenny Bridges. However, because at that time there was no bridge, only a ford with meadows surrounding it, it was called the Battle of Fenny Meadows. The country folk were armed only with billhooks and staves while the king's forces, besides being well-armed, were assisted by foreign mercenaries who were astonished at the fight put up by our west-countrymen. Recently I heard that it is said locally that on a moonlight night, if you stand on the bridge, you can see horsemen plunging about in the meadows, up to their hocks in blood.

At Hound Tor, not long ago, someone was driving along the road by Hedgebarton where there is a single avenue of old beech trees. These were in black shade for the moon was bright, and the driver saw a man in Cavalier costume walk out from the shadows into the moonlit road and vanish.

Quite a number of sites, noted for a horrible murder, martyrdom or battle, are marked by indelible bloodstains. Where these occur on plaster walls I understand they merely indicate the presence of iron oxide in the stone behind, so no amount of scrubbing or renewal of the plaster will remove them! In 1964 a correspondent from Stoke Fleming wrote to me. She lived at Southcombe Farm there, where a field of theirs called Battlefield sloped down to a stream and hedge, marking the boundary to their property. Some strangers visited her one day and pointed out that the pebbles in the brook were coloured red and explained that this was because 'the Danes' had fought a battle here and that the blood-letting of that event had permanently coloured the stones in the water!

Phantom Houses

Some books on Devon refer to 'phantom houses', which are only seen occasionally. Elliott O'Donnell, in his *Haunted Britain*, mentioned one cottage within walking distance of Chagford, which was so charming that two lady visitors who came upon it asked to have rooms there the following summer, as the accommodation was at present fully booked. Staying again in Chagford the following summer, they looked for the delightful cottage, but it was just not there. The locals told them that there were cottages in that part that only manifested themselves every ten or twelve years. Similarly J. Ll. W. Page, in his *The Rivers of Devon* (1893), told of three girls lost near Buckfastleigh who found a cottage by the roadside. It was dusk and there was a light in the cottage, and through the window they saw an old man and woman seated on a bench by the fire. They had no sooner taken this in than the cottage vanished and they were in darkness. All that could be seen next day were a few stones marking the foundations. The phenomenon was quite well known locally; 'the Phantom Cottage of the Moor', when solid, had a nasty reputation of vague but evil goings-on.

But these are not confined to Dartmoor. A friend riding through Doccombe near Moretonhampstead suddenly saw a large old manor house and garden behind an ordinary field-gate. She knew perfectly well that there was no such place and she went to considerable pains to check the possibilities, but there was absolutely no reason whatever to believe there had ever been such a mansion in Doccombe.

At Cadeleigh, near Tiverton, I have heard there is a house which appears three times only in a year; as my informant remarked dryly, if these appearances were timed to evade rates demands, what a desirable residence!

A further strange happening occurred at Stoke Fleming. Two ladies saw the 'phantom Harleston Manor' here in 1939. One of them wrote to me in 1965:

'We lived at Start House about one mile from Slapton village. Parts of the house were several hundred years old and it was completely in the country and at the end of the road. A small lane, only a footpath now, continued to Kingsbridge, about five miles away. In the old days this had been the pack-horse way to Kingsbridge, and farmers cleaning it from time to time found it to have a hard bottom, possibly cobbled. This lane led over the small river, past Battleford, entirely unpopulated except for an odd farm or two. Start House stood on high ground with the small river which ran through our property, in the valley. This valley continued with the path on the high ground, and the country on the other side of the valley sloping up through the trees.

'It was about a mile from Start House down the lane and in the woods that both my sister and I saw the phantom house. It was on a November afternoon in 1939, rather misty and damp. We had only lived in Start House for about a year and this was my sister's second visit. Both our husbands were serving in the army in France.

'I had noticed often that there were signs of an old orchard in the valley, and we had felt that there might have been a house there once. On this particular afternoon we stopped and leant over a farm gate to admire the view which was very beautiful. Suddenly my sister said to me: "I thought you said that there was no house here", and I looked across the valley, and there in the trees was a great manor house. It had big arched doors through which I half expected to see horsemen riding out in medieval costume. . . . As we watched in amazement more buildings appeared at the side of the house in the trees.

'You ask how I knew it was not real? Well, of course I knew the country so well, having walked there dozens of times, and I knew there was no house there. Also it did not *look* real. It is difficult to explain, for although the house was perfect, yet it had no substance. That is the best description that I can give. We saw no people, although we longed for the great doors to open and for people to ride out.

'As we talked and watched, perhaps for five minutes, the house gradually faded away.

'When my husband came home on leave the following spring we walked together to the site: quite a long arduous walk as we had to cross the river and scramble through the woods on the other side. My husband was intensely interested and said he had never seen a more wonderful site for a house. Also it was obvious from the levelled area – on which grew lovely grass, quite different from the surrounding country – that a house had been there. It looked right down the valley to the sea, and also up other valleys.

'Another interesting point is that several people living in Start House before us and also in the house on the other side of the lane had heard, at intervals, horses galloping down the lane. Although they had gone to look no one had ever seen the horses, only heard them go past. No doubt they came from my "ghost" house.'

Now, here again, as at Doccombe, we have an apparent throw-back to a non-existent manor house. There evidently had been some kind of habitation, but as far as I know, there has never been a large manor house on this wooded spot.

Another curious vision of a past landscape was reported in the *Journal of the Society for Psychical Research* for 1947 (vol. xxxiv, pp. 74 *et seq.*), though the account had been written down in 1940. Again, this occurred on the coast not far east of Stoke Fleming and Slapton. In March of 1938, a Mr Bates was walking on the cliff path above the little cove called Mansands between Churston Ferrers and Dartmouth. In front of him spread a wide vista of fields and his path lay across these. He stepped over a stile and found himself falling over the edge of the cliff. The meadows in front of him had vanished for they were non-existent. Had he seen the landscape as it once was, and it had eroded like the coastline a little further west at Beesands and Hallsands? If so, then to what period in time had he been wafted? And by whose viewpoint had he suddenly been invaded?

Reginald de Mohun

The saintly Reginald de Mohun was a thirteenth-century benefactor of Torre (now part of Torquay) and the founder of Newenham Abbey, now just over the border in Dorset. Reginald died in his house at Torre in 1257 and was buried in the abbey church he had founded. The learned friar who prepared him for death, having retired to his room:

'... during a short slumber, dreamed that he ... beheld a venerable person attired in white, conducting a boy more radiant than the sun and vested in a robe brighter than crystal, from the baptismal font towards the altar. On enquiring whose beautiful child this was, the person answered, "This is the soul of the venerable Reginald de Mohun."'

Three days later Mohun died, and as was the custom was buried by the High Altar. The Register of the Abbey which recounts this dream adds that when, seventy-five years later, in 1333, the pavement was disturbed, the body of the old man was found to be incorrupt and exuding a fragrant odour.

The 'Dream Church'

When I was a child the Reverend John Sturgess Martin was the Vicar of Coffinswell, a parish of about three hundred souls a few miles from Newton Abbot. His brother, the Reverend William Keble Martin, was Vicar of Dartington, a family living since the Martins were closely related to the Champernownes. The two brothers exchanged their livings, and for most of my childhood William was at Coffinswell (where my father was the sole churchwarden) and also served as Archpriest of Haccombe, in which anachronistic capacity he owed direct allegiance to the Archbishop of Canterbury. He spent much of his leisure looking out rare plants and painting them. I can remember him doing this at Barton Hall with my mother's paint-box. We little

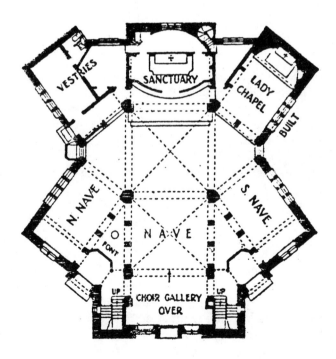

knew what fame he would achieve in old age when his great book was published: *The Concise British Flora in Colour*, 1965! We greatly admired his meticulous work, but in those days colour printing was not capable of producing such a vast work at a commercially possible price.

While he was at Coffinswell, he was asked to take on a huge new council house estate at Milber, near Newton Abbot, just off the Torquay main road. The district made do with a wooden Mission room from 1930 till a permanent church could be built. In his charming autobiography *Over the Hills* . . ., 1968, he has told how early one morning in March 1931 he dreamed he was preaching in a church with no chancel but an apse in which the altar stood. In front of him were three aisles converging, fanlike, on the altar, so that everyone in the congregation had a direct view of it. Mr Martin was thrilled with the idea and drew a rough sketch which he sent to his architect brother, and so the project of the 'Dream Church' was born, though owing to money shortage and the war, the church was only completed in 1962. Keble Martin died in 1970 in his 93rd year.

Pixies

Pixies present a difficult problem. What on earth are they? On the one hand, like fairies, they are usually said to have existed long ago but not now. On the other hand we still occasionally hear of people seeing them in modern times. My own mother used to see them when she was young, but only when she was alone and in a rather dreamy, dissociated mood. I well remember when we were camping at Postbridge in the 1920s she reported seeing a strange figure wandering at the top of Drift Lane. It was tall and thin and dressed in green, rather indefinite garments. What struck her was its air of melancholy. She had seen pixies on other occasions when as a very young woman she had walked round the cliffs surrounding Watcombe Bay, near Torquay. Then she had recently come from London. It is not only superstitious countryfolk (if there are any!) who see pixies: the most sophisticated townies can be confronted with these mysterious beings. A friend of mine, a brigadier's wife, used to see them on Dartmoor quite frequently, especially in the little valleys round the edge of the moor, where tiny streams trickle down

Chudleigh Rocks

between moss-covered rocks. She was sure they avoided the forestry plantations.

Numerous theories have been suggested to explain them, such as that they are the decadent remnant of a prehistoric race or their ghosts. Or they are diminished pagan deities, or, in Victorian folklore, the spirits of unbaptised babies hanging around in accordance with the grim old teaching that if you were not baptised you could never enter heaven, but if you were not actually wicked you would not enter hell either. Thus you dangled between heaven and hell in a kind of amoral limbo as a lost spirit outside the pale of Christian society.

The aboriginal theory is somewhat weakened by the occasional sightings of little dark men dressed in skins who have been spotted crawling out of holes and hut circles; they are not in the least like pixies, which rather spoils the old Breton ideas about changelings. They believed that the race of pixies was so diminished and feeble that they needed to improve their stock by kidnapping human babies and small children and placing one of their feeblest specimens in the cradle to bamboozle the human mother till her own was far away. Of course the explanation is very different from our point of view. Only a couple of generations ago ailing children, perhaps autistic, lacking in certain vitamins, or suffering from a metabolic abnormality (one produces pointed ears and is significantly named 'leprechaunism') were deemed to be changelings. One South Devon village had inhabitants who seemed of less than normal size and were believed to be the victims of a pixy raid and so were all changelings. Even in Victorian times Chudleigh women tied their babies into their cots to prevent a similar mishap.

Chudleigh Rocks were supposed to be a favourite home of 'the little people'. This is a wooded glen between cliffs of limestone, honeycombed with caves, an inner cul-de-sac being known as 'the Pixies' Parlour'. These caves and rocks are a popular if tough challenge to rock-climbers and speleologists. Down the glen flows the Katebrook (or Kidbrook) to join the River Teign near the site of the old Station and Bridge Cottage.

By the Rocks once lived a gamekeeper with his wife and two small children. One morning the elder child, having been dressed first, wandered off and was lost. Her parents searched high and low for days, with the assistance of neighbours and even bloodhounds, but no sign of her could be found. Eventually two young men nutting near the cottage came upon the little girl. She had no clothes on but appeared perfectly well and happy and not even hungry, and was sitting playing with her toes. It was assumed that the pixies had abducted her, but why they returned such a hearty specimen is not explained! This story was told by a local inhabitant to Lady Rosalind Northcote.

Our forbears believed that before the Reformation pixies feared only holy water and the sound of church bells and kept firmly away from churches, but that after the Reformation they departed altogether because the clergy were more learned; on the other hand they still lingered near ruined monasteries because the 'old church' had at least recognised their existence, along with a heap of other beliefs condemned by the Puritans as superstitions. Herrick indeed thought that if the fairies and pixies had any religion at all it was 'papistical'. But, of course, this was purely a matter of prejudice. What is plain is that pixies were either pre-Christian or sub-Christian and quite amoral, unformed beings without human identity, melancholy because they were without the responsibility or promise of human privilege; outcasts, in fact, seeking human comfort and assurance, like animals or like ourselves in our most primitive, subconscious aspect.

The late Mrs Rosalind Heywood's *The Infinite Hive* contains a most thought-provoking passage, inspired by her experience during a visit to Okehampton on the northern side of Dartmoor. She did not see pixies, but, she said, she became aware of a single consciousness expressed through visible things; as she wrote: 'Also through myriads of invisible entities which form the inner life of the wild. . . . I know that I have brushed the fringe of a group consciousness as real as my own, though one from which "civilised" man has cut himself adrift, so that it shrinks from him as an invader, coarse, vulgar and arrogant, imperceptive and cruel.' To begin with, Mrs Heywood felt that these beings hated her, but when she came to understand their viewpoint she felt a deep peace and harmony.

So, in some way pixies are merely the untamed and playful part of ourselves, which no doubt is why children often see them. A member of a Women's Institute near Tiverton told me that her grandson, aged about four, often sees them. He has seen them sitting and swinging on the fir trees behind his home. They wear hats of red or sometimes blue, which his grandmother thought fitted his particular mood!

So the subject is a complex one and we could discuss indefinitely the activities of pixies down through the ages. Apart from dancing in the moonlight and teasing mortals, they could be most useful. They threshed the corn for farmers and swept the kitchens for their wives in return for a bowl of cream, which was left outside and always cleared by morning.

They also disciplined the farm servants. Hence William Browne, the Tavistock poet of Stuart times, says that the Fairy Queen:

> '. . . did command her Elves,
> To pinch those Maides that had not swept their shelves. . . .
> And for the Maide that had perform'd each thing
> She in the Water-payle bad leave a Ring.'

One hears of none of this nowadays. I suppose they just do not know what to make of combine harvesters and vacuum sweepers, and they would probably feel cheated if offered the strange concoction that now passes for clotted cream.

This happy arrangement has been long neglected in our times. Yet it was not long ago – actually in the 1930s – that haymakers in North

Devon would slop a little cider on the ground or throw out a few crumbs as a libation to the 'little people'; and as far as I know some folk when picking apples in the autumn still leave a few on the ground for their invisible friends: 'pixy-worting' it is called.

Pixies appear to have something in common with poltergeists, especially in 'pixy riding' which still occurs. A cousin of mine at Chudleigh Knighton ran a small riding stable. She told me that many a time she had gone to the stable in the early morning and found the ponies' manes all knotted and tangled quite inexplicably, and the ponies themselves exhausted and sweaty. The stable doors had been carefully locked so that there was no chance the horses had been used by humans.

Being 'pixy-led' is a curious but by no means unknown phenomenon even in this century. I have recorded several instances in recent years. You are on a journey, probably on foot, along a well-known route which may lead through a field. You suddenly become totally disorientated and unable to proceed. 'I were all twirled around. I didn't knaw where I was tu. I were proper pixy-led,' said a Postbridge woman coming across from one farm to another. And a Kenn woman was pixy-led walking home from Exeter. It usually happens at night, but it can happen in broad daylight with distant landmarks perfectly visible. The standard cure is to turn pockets or coats inside out. A woman I met about twenty years ago told me that when she first visited Devon her hostess took her for a drive round the edge of Dartmoor. Pretty soon they lost themselves in a maze of lanes. Not a signpost could they spot and after a while they lost all sense of direction. At length the driver stopped the car, got out, turned her coat inside out and struggled back into it, remarking to her astonished passenger: '*Now* we'll soon find our way.' – and they did, at once.

In Elizabethan times the Fitz family owned estates round Tavistock and Okehampton. Sir John Fitz of Fitzford, a friend of Drake, was an astrologer; one day he and his wife were riding on the moor and found themselves hopelessly lost. After wandering for a long time they came upon a spring of clear water. They dismounted and drank from it – suddenly they recognised their surroundings and found their way back easily. In gratitude Sir John had a granite surround built round the spring and a cross placed by it. The story is told of two springs, both known as Fitz's Well: one is near Okehampton, by the military road which penetrates the moor, and

Fitz's Well near Okehampton

the other is at Princetown, now within the precincts of the Prison. This cross bears the initials 'I.F.' and the date 1568 and is thought to be the original spring of the legend, but I suspect Sir John was responsible for both structures. He and Drake shared a common interest in the problems of public water supplies.

Pixies were generally thought to live underground, emerging from caves or crevices in the rocks at night-time to dance wildly till dawn, compelling any passers-by to join in the dance, however exhausted, and even forcing itinerant fiddlers or pipers to play for them. With the first beam of sunrise they sank down through the clitter to their subterranean dormitories. This is the only dwelling hinted at and naturally enough it appeals to the promoters of the 'Hollow Earth' theory who would like to postulate an aboriginal race 'gone underground' for untold thousands of years, developing independently and only waiting their time to take over the above-ground world. But this hardly sounds like pixies.

Sealed Rooms – and Their Occupants

In my wanderings in Devon I occasionally come upon mysterious rooms with no windows and a strongly locked door. One house, I noted, had an odd-shaped hall, into which the main staircase descended. It was square in shape, very high, with a skylight; the landing was a balcony passage going round two sides at first floor level. It looked as though this had once been part of a first-floor room right over the hall. My host assured me that this had once been the case. 'It was a windowless room,' he explained, 'in which was placed any member of the family who was insane.'

This was a new idea to me; I had always thought that the incarceration of poor Mrs Rochester in *Jane Eyre* was an unusual procedure, but it appears to have been quite common in big houses before the advent of nursing homes, but the mind boggles at the possibilities of malpractice of various kinds, not to mention horrible complications.

One windowless room was discovered in Powderham Castle, on the ground floor, just behind the hall. In the last century, the owners

Powderham Castle

noticed a strong oak door that was locked. They wanted to open up the room that must lie behind and build a new staircase. With much difficulty they got the door open. Behind it was a windowless apartment as they knew there must be. In it was a bedstead with a skeleton on it. There was not a clue as to the corpse's identity, no scrap of evidence or rumour as to who it could have been or why it was locked up, or how it met its death or when. All they could do was to give it Christian burial, and continue with the planned alterations.

Another long-dead skeleton was found in a secret room in Chambercombe Manor, near Ilfracombe. The late James Turner (*Ghosts in the South West*, 1973) heard that it was the remains of a young woman murdered by local wreckers. One legend held that this was Kate Oatway, the daughter of their leader, who left her in this room to starve.

An elderly correspondent from Yorkshire once wrote to me about various North Devon traditions he had heard when living there as a young man. About the old Hall of Weare Gifford on the River Torridge, between Great Torrington and Bideford he said:

'In the Hall there is said to be a room in the upper floor which has been bricked up. A young woman had a certain disease (not specified) and in accordance with custom the room with her in it was "eliminated". Recently a visitor took a dog to this floor, and the animal on coming to the door of the room appeared panic-stricken and ran away, looking back frequently as though there was someone there.'

My correspondent added he had no idea whether there really was such a room in the Hall, but a similar explanation might account for the previous example at Powderham.

Sometimes it could be a priest's hole used during the period after the Reformation when to be a Roman Catholic priest was a crime punishable by death. Wealthy recusant families tried to protect priests by having secret rooms into which they hurried them when there was a raid by local magistrates. Many such hiding-places have been discovered in recent times when alterations are being made. Not far from Beer is the charming Tudor house of Bovey. At some time this belonged to Lord Clinton and it is said that when some repairs were being carried out on the roof, a portion of this was found to be partitioned off to form a little room. In it was an old chair (but no skeleton). Upon Lord Clinton being consulted he requested that the

Bovey House, Beer

chair be removed and the room sealed. Immediately a flood of poltergeist activity started up which only ceased when the chair was replaced.

There was also a tunnel, leading from behind a panel in a first-storey room down to the cliff. It has caved in long ago and is impassable. This was for the use of smugglers at a time when they used Bovey House as their depot. There also used to be rumours of ghosts, no doubt promulgated by Jack Rattenbury, the famous smuggler, to frighten people away. No one has seen the flicker of a haunting for many generations.

Haunted Waters

I have no doubt that there must be phantom ships round our two coasts but oddly I have no note of any in my records, though there are certainly ghostly figures of various kinds here and there. Tantrobobus, a giant bogey, is known on the North Devon coast and has been heard of around the Brixham area in the south. I have never heard what he is supposed to do, though he has been a useful 'threat' for mothers to scare their children into good behaviour. 'Q', in his *Troy Town*, mentions a 'Cankobobus' who seems to be a Cornish variant.

A rather more sinister figure is 'Old White-hat' or 'Jack the Whithat' who haunted the southern point of Braunton Burrows and hailed the ferry coming in from Appledore, and everyone was scared of him. At other times he tries to spin ropes out of sand and probably was based on a real man, since apparently he has descendants living in Bideford. He could be recognised at a distance by the great white hat he wears with a lantern attached to it. It sounds almost like a memory of the old wrecker's dodge, of tying a lantern to a horse's head and leading it along the cliff, which is alleged to have been done at Morthoe; here the ghostly horse can still be seen trying to mislead ships at sea.

Some years ago I heard a curious story from a young married man at Barnstaple. He said that one fine summer evening he and his fiancée took a picnic supper up to the Valley of Rocks at Lynton and sat on the cliffs looking out over a smooth blue sea. They became aware of music coming from under the cliff – singing it was, a lovely choral tune. They crept to the edge and looked down, thinking, of course, it must come from a holiday boatload of people, but they could see nothing at all. So I said: 'It must have been seals in a cave under the cliffs,' but the young man replied: 'No. I could hear the words.' But he could not remember them or identify the song. So I still reckon it was seals, who will sometimes sing together like this. Ruth L. Tongue, the great Somerset folklorist, has heard them off Exmoor, and they have been heard at Hartland also.

But to return to water spirits. It was commonly believed in olden times that all rivers were controlled by a powerful god or goddess who had to be kept sweet by offerings of various kinds, and their very name was to be avoided as sacred; and they bitterly resented having a

The Valley of Rocks, Lynton

bridge built over them, thus enabling mortals to bypass the flood without ceremony. So there are quantities of superstitions and legends reflecting these ideas that survive to this day. Some rivers demand an annual toll of a human life. The Tamar is one such and so is the River Dart – hence the old couplet:

'River of Dart, River of Dart!
Every year thou claimest a heart.'

And indeed lives are easily lost on that beautiful but treacherous little river. When I was young I can remember people discussing a recent accident and saying, almost with relief: 'Well, the Dart has had her victim for *this* year!'

Another river with an eery reputation is the Wulf, a tributary of the Tamar that runs through part of West Devon. Baring-Gould wrote of it that once the only access to the village of Broadwoodwidger was by a ford in this stream which was liable to flood violently. It was supposed to be haunted by a gigantic but kindly spirit who obligingly carried people across! He thought there might be a confusion of St Christopher (whose picture was on a fresco in the church) with an older memory of Thor, who was often described as wading in deep water.

There is a sinister pool on Dartmoor on a lonely hillside east of Burrator. This is Crasiwell (or Crazywell or Clakeywell) Pool, locally believed to be bottomless, though actually it is merely a flooded tin-mine and only fifteen feet deep. But being on a hillside it is surrounded on three sides by extremely high banks which make it look very black and horrific. People are said to avoid passing it at night because you are liable to hear a loud voice announcing the name of the next person in the parish to die. Though really I cannot imagine anyone in their senses passing that remote spot in the dark. Sometimes fearful howls as of a soul in torment are heard. Someone wrote a ballad about an ancient legend attached to the place. This refers to the miserable Piers Gaveston who, in one of his periods of disfavour at court, was supposed to be wandering on Dartmoor. A famous prophetess lived near and he made an appointment to meet her at Crasiwell Pool to have his fortune told. The pronouncement when it was uttered was as ambiguous as any that came out of Delphi:

'Fear not, thou favourite of a king:
Thy humbled head shall soon be high.'

And so it was: decapitated at Warwick, on a hill top.

The most famous of all is Cranmere Pool which lies in the centre of the northern half of Dartmoor in a hollow of the great upland morass. From it the little River Okement trickles northwards and gives its name to Okehampton. It appears to have been famous in medieval times though for what reason is not stated. However, certainly by the end of the eighteenth century onwards it was known as an abode for unwanted spooks and in the Victorian guidebooks tales were told of individual ghosts being hurled into the black waters: one of these was a mysterious being known as Benjie Geare. This was the spirit of a former Mayor of Okehampton, Benjamin Gayer, about whom we know remarkably little. He was mayor five times and died in 1701; his memorial tablet in Latin adorns the vestry in the parish church but his grave is not marked – there is an altar tomb to a Benjamin Geare, but the date is 1645, indicating an earlier generation. No record of his reputation has come down to us, but tradition holds that he haunted Okehampton so badly that the vicar was constrained to lay him, which he did by taking him out to Cranmere Pool. Provided only with a sieve he was ordered to bale out the pool. After many years he wearied of the impossible task and thought out a cunning plan to end it. He waited till a flock of sheep wandered by, caught one, killed and skinned it and spread this across the sieve. He baled out the pool at such a speed that all Okehampton was flooded, and he returned to the town in triumph. Now the inhabitants really despaired of getting rid of him, so they appealed to the archdeacon for advice. Thirteen of the local clergy all had a turn at trying to control Benjie, but to no purpose until it was the turn of the thirteenth parson who addressed the ghost in Arabic. This finished the startled spook who exclaimed: 'Now thou art come I must be gone,' and was turned into a black pony that could be controlled. A new bridle was fixed on his head, and a boy, fortified by Holy Communion, was ordered to ride the pony out to Cranmere Pool and, once there, to dismount, remove the bridle and walk swiftly back to Okehampton without once looking back. All went well until the bridle was slipped off, but the lad, overcome by natural curiosity, glanced back. The demon pony took a tremendous leap into the pool and disappeared in the depth, but one of his flying hooves caught the boy in the face and blinded him in one eye. So Okehampton was relieved of the haunting, but legend claims that Benjie still haunts the pool as a black pony or a black dwarf, and if you wish to avoid Okehampton being plagued with a stupendous thunderstorm you must not walk round a table three times saying:

'Benjie Geare, Benjie Geare!
If thou art near, do thou appear!'

Some wells and springs are said to be haunted by ghostly White Ladies: I can think of only two in Devon. Baring-Gould mentions one ghost of a woman, buried near a well at Coffinswell, Newton Abbot. Every New Year's Day, just after midnight, she arises from her grave and takes one cock-stride towards the churchyard. When she arrives there eventually she may rest.

Near Bampton, on the Exmoor border, there is a farm called Holwell. The road there once had a pond beside it which was filled in, so the belief is, because it was haunted by a White Woman, and the villagers would not pass it at night. I have not heard of any definite sighting.

It has been suggested that these 'White Women', so often reported from notable springs all over the country, may be the ghostly echoes of once venerated water nymphs. Many holy wells are dedicated to Our Lady, hence the local names 'Ladywell' or even 'Ladewell' or

'Lidwell'. In Devon we have an exceptional number of these, probably to absorb and cancel out the memory of a local nymph.

Finally, here is a very minor haunting: a senior boy at Tiverton Grammar School told me about it in 1970. He came from Kentisbeare, near Cullompton. Quite close to Bradfield House is Pixies' Pool. There is a road near it, and at the full of the moon a farmer can be seen riding a cart horse which is pulling a roller up and down the road.

Cutty Dyer

One of Ashburton's most distinguished sons was Professor John Satterley, FRS, who died in 1963. From quite a modest origin he rose to be a famous physicist at the University of Toronto and a popular figure on Canadian television. I only knew him in old age as he was retiring. He and his wife made a habit of returning to England for the summer vacation, timing a Devon visit to coincide with the annual meetings of the Devonshire Association every June. He was a striking figure, tall, handsome with fine white hair. Despite his distinguished career, he retained his delightful west-country accent and, his memory being crystal clear, was able to inform and entertain us with some exceptional local traditions and stories from his childhood.

When he was young, Professor Satterley believed firmly in 'one, Cutty Dyer who was supposed to live under the arches which spanned the River Yeo behind North Street (in Ashburton) and who – so our parents said – would catch us if we ventured too far. . . . From Dawe's Mill the leat went underground before joining the river. This dark channel was a favourite abode of Cutty Dyer.' He has told me of the fearful roaring noise the water made when it was released from the leat and the pent-up water joined the river, and how all the boys ran, imagining it was Cutty Dyer bellowing for his prey!

In early Victorian times there were other memories of the ogre. Drunks reeling home at night represented 'the being as a giant wading in the water, with eyes as large as saucers, trying to pull them in'. This image must date back to a period before the bridge was built and wayfarers had to cross by the ford which may have been guarded over by a wooden carving of St Christopher: there are two entries in the Churchwardens' Accounts in the sixteenth century about buying a block of wood for this purpose. It might be that St Christopher somehow got confused with the river ogre, but oddly there does seem once to have been a local miller called Christopher Dyer, and there is a bridge further up the Yeo called Cuttyford Bridge, so it looks as though the original monster was first confused with St Christopher by drunks at night-time, and then with the miller.

When I talked about Cutty Dyer to a local group in 1971 I was assured that no such entity was known in Ashburton, and my quotation of Professor Satterley was received with some scepticism. However, a few days later, my audience changed their tune, for a relative of one of them was a nurse at a nearby hospital. She worked in the geriatric ward. One of her patients was a very senile man who lay passively in his bed muttering inaudibly to himself. She listened to him one day and found he was muttering about Cutty Dyer!

A very unexpected clue came later from Somerset. Ruth Tongue told me she has met old women who had been born in Ashburton and married Somerset men. They have told her they do not like going out at night, especially if it involves crossing a bridge over a river 'because summat like Cutty Dyer'll come up behind 'ee'. Enquiring who Cutty Dyer might be, the reply is always of a vague robber that cuts people's throats from behind, drinks their blood and throws the bodies into the river. They speak of this as a present possibility and dislike crossing *any* bridges at night, though that over the River Tone at Taunton has been mentioned specifically. And there was a very old man in a blind people's home in Taunton; he had been born in Ashburton but was now very alone and withdrawn, and had hardly been known to speak to anyone. In 1972, just before he died he suddenly spoke up:

'Dawn't 'ee go down the riverzide:
Cutty Dyer du abide.
Cutty Dyer ain't no gude:
Cutty Dyer'll drink yer blood!'

Further Reading

There is no definitive book of Devon ghost stories. The selection I have given here comes from a very wide selection of miscellaneous sources: some have not appeared in print before. Most of my material has been published by the Devonshire Association in their annual *Transactions* which include my Folklore Reports for the past thirty years. *Devon and Cornwall Notes and Queries* contains a lot of ghost material though it is mainly of the legendary variety. Numerous old writers have recorded stories of the supernatural, notably Mrs Bray, S. Baring-Gould, F. J. Snell and William Crossing. It would make tedious reading to include every reference but I have tried to indicate the main ones. As regards recent sightings there is no better source than the local press: hardly a month passes without a poltergeist or ghost being reported.

Some recent books dealing with Devon ghosts are:

Theo Brown: *The Fate of the Dead*, pub. for the Folklore Society by D. S. Brewer and Littlefield & Rowman, 1979.

Judy Chard: *Devon Mysteries*, Bossiney Books, 1979.

J. R. W. Coxhead: *Legends of Devon*, The Western Press, 1954.

J. R. W. Coxhead: *Devon Traditions and Fairy Tales*, Raleigh Press, 1957.

J. R. W. Coxhead: *Ghosts in Devon*, Town & Country Press, 1972.

James Turner: *Ghosts in the South West*, David & Charles, 1973.

Shades and Spectres: A Guide to Devon Hauntings, compiled by the Devon Folk Register for the Exeter City Museums Service, 1978.

Sources of Illustrations

We are grateful to the following for permission to use pictures:

The National Portrait Gallery.
The Council and Hon. Editor, The Devonshire Association.
The Librarians at The Devon & Exeter Institution; the West Country Studies Library, Exeter Central Library.

Other prints are from the private collection of the author.

Photographs are by J. Brooks, P. M. Bourke, Hilary Vivian, and the author.